A History of Penistone and District

A HISTORY OF
PENISTONE
AND DISTRICT

David Hey

Wharncliffe Books

Dedication
For my sister, Barbara

First Published in 2002 by
Wharncliffe Books
an imprint of
Pen and Sword Books Limited,
47 Church Street, Barnsley,
South Yorkshire. S70 2AS

Copyright © David Hey 2002

For up-to-date information on other titles produced under the
Wharncliffe imprint, please telephone or write to:

Wharncliffe Books
FREEPOST
47 Church Street
Barnsley
South Yorkshire S70 2BR
Telephone (24 hours): 01226 - 734555

ISBN: 1-903425-21-2

A CIP catalogue record of this book is available from the
British Library

Front Cover illustration: *Whitsuntide procession, Bridge Street, Penistone* (Old Barnsley).
Illustration to the right, Contents page: *High Street, Penistone. The narrow main street captured by Joshua Biltcliffe in*
the horse-and-cart era.

Printed in the United Kingdom by
CPI UK

CONTENTS

✠

PREFACE

This book is based on lectures that I have given over the years to the Penistone branch of the WEA and other societies. I have not written all that I know about my native district; rather, I have tried to show how the various places within Penistone's ancient parish developed and how the countryside changed, how some families stayed here for centuries and how much history there is still to see in our everyday surroundings.

I also want to show how oral history and personal memories can contribute to a richer understanding of local history. I am an academic historian, trained to read and interpret a wide range of documents from the medieval period onwards, but I am also a local man who spent his childhood in the 1940s in what was then a remote hamlet, two or three miles to the west of Penistone, where life was not very different from what it had been for several generations. The changes in the last fifty years have been so considerable that the way of life that I was familiar with, now seems incredibly old-fashioned. I have used these memories in both the opening and closing chapters, but lest it seems that I have amazing powers of recall I should explain that in the early 1960s I made notes from conversations with my mother about my childhood home and that many years later John Moore kindly talked to me about his memories of working alongside my father in Sledbrook Colliery.

The Penistone district is exceptionally fortunate in having scores of old photographs taken by Joshua Biltcliffe and his son, John Thomas Biltcliffe. On our daily walk home from Penistone Grammar School we often stopped to gaze at the selection of these in the shop window in Bridge Street. Those reproduced here are from my own collection, many of them donated by the late Joe Windle or bought from Chris Sharp's *Old Barnsley* stall. Some views are familiar, but many are published for the first time. Dr Sheila Edwards took the photographs of the two guide stoops and of Bullhouse chapel from across the former railway. The aerial views are printed by courtesy of Meridian Airmaps Ltd.

My great-great-grandfather, John Hey, moved from Shelley to Thurlstone two hundred years ago and many of his descendants still live in the Penistone district. I remain deeply attached to the place. After a recent lecture in Sheffield to people from far and wide, someone asked where my unusual accent came from. I invited them to guess and, to my astonishment, a woman said, 'Well, I think you're from Penistone'. It turned out that she lived in Stockport and knew someone who had moved there from Penistone as a teenager some forty years ago and who sounded just like me. My local roots go very deep and it has been a labour of love to write about the places that I know so well.

I would like to thank Brian Elliott and the staff of Wharncliffe Books for all their help with this publication.

David Hey
June 2002

Chapter One

The View from Catshaw

Two or three miles to the west of Penistone a row of thirteen elegant windfarms turn slowly on the skyline, glinting in the sun. They are a striking sight from afar and can be seen from the M1 motorway many miles to the east. On coming over Gilbert Hill from Langsett, the traveller's immediate reaction is to admire the surreal, dignified way that they generate electricity without contaminating the atmosphere, but soon their insistent presence disturbs our contemplation and begins to irritate the eye. Outsiders may remember them as the sole attraction in this rugged Pennine landscape, but for those who live in this remote valley that was my childhood home they are an unwelcome intrusion, a visual pollution that can be ignored only by turning one's back on them to gaze towards the Pennine moors.

My regret at this change to the scenery that I loved so well as a boy in the 1940s is tempered by the personal recognition of the advantages of modern technology. We had no electricity at Catshaw, nor any gas. Our light came from a paraffin lamp and candles, our water had to be heated in pans on the coal fire, and our toilet was a privy midden across the farmyard. I would willingly have traded these in for some spoiling of the scenery. The old adage 'beauty is in

The modern windfarms seen from Hartcliff. Catshaw is in the middle distance, beyond Bullhouse, which has a solitary windfarm.

the eye of the beholder' comes readily to my mind when I contemplate the view from Catshaw, for this is not a pretty or charming landscape. Its value is apparent only to those of us who have learned to enjoy the rather bare, windswept fringes of the Pennines. Even its admirers shudder at the memory of the bleakness of the harsh winter of 1947. The valley is beautiful only on a summer's day.

The valley had been opened up to the technology of the outside world twice before. In 1741 the old track along which salt had been brought since time immemorial from Cheshire over Woodhead and across the county boundary at Saltersbrook towards Salter Hill and the markets at Barnsley, Doncaster and Rotherham had been converted into a turnpike road. Two hundred years later, however, the steady trickle of traffic through Millhouse Green was still insignificant when compared with the continuous flow of today. The other important change came in 1845 with the completion of the Woodhead Tunnel (at that time the longest in Britain) and the opening of the Sheffield to Manchester railway four years later. A bridge across the turnpike road led into a deep cutting by Bullhouse Chapel and to a small station at Hazlehead Bridge. Steam trains took a steady supply of coal from the South Yorkshire coalfield to Lancashire and Cheshire. The 'fish train' came the other way late at night from Liverpool on its way to Harwich. So important was the line that in 1954 it became the first in the country to be electrified. Now it lies abandoned, converted in part into a long-distance walk across the Pennines.

This then is not a timeless, unchanging landscape, ancient in parts though it undoubtedly appears. In many ways the upper Don valley is now a more attractive place than it was when I was a boy. The houses and cottages are in far better condition. They are clean, bright, well-equipped and maintained to a much higher standard than was possible during the Second World War and the post-war years of austerity. These old buildings have been restored by some of the old families that I knew in the 1940s or by incomers who commute daily to Sheffield, Barnsley or Huddersfield. When I was a boy only Mr Marsden of Bullhouse Hall worked in Sheffield. I did not know anybody else who travelled to work more than the four or five miles by bus to Samuel Fox's steelworks at Stocksbridge. Most people walked to work or took a short bus ride to Hoyland's umbrella works at Millhouse or to the clay pipe works and coal pit of the Hepworth Iron Company at Crowedge.

Flint tools and stone axes found on the moors and the prehistoric earthworks at Denby Common, Langsett and Roughbirchworth that are marked on old Ordnance Survey maps as 'Castle Hill' or 'Castle

Dyke' are our only clues to the earliest settlers in this district. We simply do not know how far back in time the present pattern of settlement began to take shape. Many of the farms and hamlets in the old parish of Penistone (which extended over the moors to the county boundary in the west) were first recorded by name in the thirteenth and fourteenth centuries when local records began, but at that time some may have already been centuries old. Carlecoates, for example, two miles further up the Don valley than Catshaw, was recorded in a thirteenth century document, but the name, meaning the cottages of the churls or free peasants, is much older than that.[1] The survival of early records is a chancy business. Catshaw was not mentioned in any existing document until 1611, when it was owned by Aymor Rich of Bullhouse Hall, but it may have had a much longer, unrecorded history before it belonged to this well-documented family.[2] It occupies exactly the sort of position – on a spur above a river – that was favoured by medieval farmers in this type of country. Five wells and a spring are marked on the first edition of the six-inch Ordnance Survey map of 1854 within convenient walking distance of the hamlet. The place-name describes a small wood or copse inhabited by wild cats, a name that must refer to an uninhabited feature of the landscape before a farm was created. Very few trees adorn the present neighbourhood, but the memory of small woods is preserved in the names of other local farms: Smallshaw, Bradshaw and Fullshaw (the small, broad and dirty woods) and Hazlehead, just across the fields to the west of Catshaw.

Catshaw occupies high ground, 850 feet above sea level, on the northern side of the River Don, whose source can be found three or four miles further west, beyond Dunford Bridge. Don was written and pronounced Dun until about 1800. Bullhouse Hall, the greatest house in these parts, stands on a steeper bank on the opposite side of the river. This fine, gabled hall, lit by mullioned windows, was built in two stages in the seventeenth century, by Sylvanus Rich (in 1655) and his son, Elkanah (in 1688). The Rich family appear in local records back in the 1370s, further up the valley at Carlecoates. William Rich, who moved from Carlecoates in 1486, was the first of eleven generations of Riches to live at Bullhouse, a line that ended in 1769 with the death of Aymor Rich.[3] For three or four hundred years the Riches had been the major landowners in the western part of Penistone parish. Junior branches of the family lived at various times in nearby farmsteads at Catshaw, Hornthwaite, Millhouse, Parkin House, Royd and Smallshaw. The Riches also owned two corn mills at Bullhouse and Thurlstone and two fulling mills for thickening and

The author's father, aged 2, at Bullhouse Lodge in 1906. The house, which was built by Elkanah Rich in 1686, has been restored by Michael and Elaine Marsden.

cleansing cloth at Millhouse and Thurlstone. They dominated that large part of Penistone parish which went under the name of Thurlstone township. My father was born in the house known as Bullhouse Lodge, which Elkanah Rich had built for his daughter in 1686, but which had become decidedly old fashioned by the early years of the twentieth century, when his father worked as a waggoner at Bullhouse Mill. The chapel that Elkanah erected at the other side of his hall played an important part in all our lives.

When Sylvanus Rich died in 1683 he left the tenancy of the farm at Catshaw to David Rich, the existing tenant. At that time, Catshaw seems to have been just one farm, though it is possible that another already existed up the slope at Catshaw Cross. Emmanuel Rich, yeoman, died at Catshaw Cross in 1719. Five years later, Abel Rich leased Catshaw Farm to James Stuart of Catshaw Cross.[4] In the lease Catshaw was named alternatively as Catshaw Whine, presumably because of the whin or gorse that must have once grown in abundance there. In 1772 the two farms were the only buildings in the present hamlet that were shown on Thomas Jeffreys's map of Yorkshire, the first large-scale map that we have.[5] Between them lay a small piece of common land known as Catshaw Green, on which a cottage was erected in the nineteenth century. Catshaw Cross takes its name from a boundary stone that has been built into the wall by the roadside. Shaws were often used as boundary markers in the foothills of the Pennines, but just what Catshaw Cross and another stone (which has long since gone) at Fullshaw Cross formed the boundary of is a bit of a puzzle. Early documents frequently refer to properties in these western parts of the parish as being in 'Thurlstone Meare', a word which meant a boundary and which was used in the Pennines to denote the rough common pastures on the edge of the moors. Perhaps the two crosses divided the inner limits of Thurlstone township from the district of the 'Meare', which stretched as far west as Saltersbrook, but in the centuries before accurate maps were drawn farms on either side of the boundary line were sometimes said to be in Thurlstone Meare. The exact limits were perhaps not well known. No other explanation for the name Catshaw Cross is evident; it certainly marked some ancient boundary or other. It was probably already old by 1647, when

The old boundary stone known as Catshaw Cross still stands by the road from Millhouse to Hazlehead.

Adam Eyre of Hazlehead Hall noted in his diary for 30 August, 'I went on foote to Catshaw crosse'.[6]

The infant River Don forms the central feature of this local landscape. Emerging from a small, wooded valley below Hazlehead Hall, it meanders around the natural spur of Bullhouse, gathering pace as it flows through the narrow gap that it has carved between two prominent ridges that converge on Thurlstone. The panoramic view looking back from Hoylandswaine Height shows how this gap defines the limit of the moorland country that lies beyond. From Catshaw the two ridges on the northern and southern skylines taper dramatically to this point, enclosing Millhouse Green and the hamlets on the hill sides within the view but hiding Penistone, the small market town and parochial centre, and obscuring most of the village of Thurlstone. To a child, Catshaw seemed a quiet, private world that was rarely visited by outsiders. At night time it was pitch dark in a way that can hardly be appreciated today when street lamps and house lights shine so strongly. The only sounds were those of the wind and of the cattle lowing in the mistal across the farmyard.

The settlement pattern that pre-dated the industrial developments of the nineteenth century can be visualised with the aid of Thomas Jefferys's map, which marks nine mills on the Don on its course through the parish of Penistone, but hardly any other buildings along the banks of the river. The older farmsteads sought drier land on the spurs that projected from the hillsides. Many of their names were recorded in medieval documents – Billcliff, Bullhouse, Ecklands, Hartcliff, Hazlehead, Hornthwaite, Langsett, Ranah, Royd, Smallshaw, Swinden and the Lee, which has given us the name of Lee Lane, are all mentioned in thirteenth or fourteenth century deeds. But other farm names were not recorded in surviving documents before the sixteenth or seventeenth centuries. Catshaw, Flash House, Illions, Middle Cliff and Softley may be as old as the other farmsteads, but as they are mostly grouped together at the end of Lee Lane perhaps they represent new settlement when the national population grew in Elizabethan times. Remoter farms, high on the hills, such as Eagle Nest (an early home of my father's elder brother, Arthur) and Daisy Hill (where my mother's brother, George Batty, was tenant) were created much later, after the Thurlstone Enclosure Award of 1816 had divided up the former commons and wastes.

Jeffreys's map marks the turnpike road coming over the moors from Boardhill and veering north at Fullshaw down the valley to Millhouse and Thurlstone. Lee Lane was not then a through road, but merely provided access to the farms at Flash House and Illions, just beyond Catshaw. The 'Slade Brook' or Sledbrook was marked on the map but as yet no settlement existed at Crowedge. The road from the *Flouch Inn* to Hazlehead Bar and on to Huddersfield was not constructed until 1821. Lee Lane was probably extended to Hazlehead Bar and across the other road to Carlecoates at the same time. The moorland farms to the west of Catshaw must have been even lonelier places in the eighteenth century than they were when I was a boy. In 1772 Catshaw was not yet a hamlet, the small village of Millhouse Green did not exist, and Thurlstone had not spread along the valley of the Don. During the early part of the nineteenth century the old farmhouse at Catshaw was extended eastwards by a downstairs living room and kitchen and an upstairs chamber that was fitted with a row of weaver's windows in the gable end. The old dual economy of the West Riding farming and weaving families that is suggested by this arrangement continued well into Victorian times, long after the new scribbling and spinning mills had been built down by the river. Hand loom weavers still lived and worked in some of the

The landscape of the Penistone district was altered dramatically by the enclosure of the commons and wastes in the early nineteenth century. These rectangular fields and the new farm of Bella Vista were created after the Thurlstone enclosure award of 1816.

Thurlstone cottages when the national census was taken in 1881.

The 6,552 acres of commons and wastes in Thurlstone township were enclosed between 1812 and 1816 by a private *Act of Parliament*. Catshaw and its immediate environs were not affected, for the fields there were already ancient enclosures. The new, rectangular fields with their straight walls and lanes are best seen over the ridge at Royd Moor or beyond the other ridge east of Hartcliff around Bella Vista, but they can also be found to the south, near Ecklands, Fullshaw, Daisy Hill and Ranah. The uncultivated wastes beyond were converted into grouse-shooting moors. Thurlstone Moors, Langsett Moors and Midhope Moors, the visual limits of my childhood world, were inaccessible to us, though I did not realise it at the time. They seemed far away and as some had been used as army training grounds during the Second World War we had heard that unexploded bombs lay scattered around. Nor did I know the gamekeepers or anyone who had worked as a beater for the men who shot grouse. The war had probably curtailed such activities. I did not ramble on the moors until I was a teenager. A walk around Langsett reservoir, on the edge of the moor, was as far as we got.

During the nineteenth century the population of Thurlstone township (of which Catshaw formed part) almost doubled from 1,096 to 2,018. Many of the new inhabitants were housed at Thurlstone or Millhouse Green but some of the old farmsteads on the hill sides attracted cottages around them and so became hamlets. Catshaw was one of these. Nearly all the cottages that I knew as a boy were built in the first half of the nineteenth century. I was born into a world that was decidedly old-fashioned, but in 1949, when I was nearly eleven years old, we moved to a new council house in Penistone, to a much busier world two or thee miles from Catshaw. Over half a century later, it is now time to write down what I have learned over the years about the history of my native parish.

Chapter Two

Church and Parish

✠

Penistone's Ancient Parish

Penistone Church is a striking landmark from every direction and is clearly the focal point of its large parish. But when we look at the shape of this ancient parish on the first edition of the six-inch Ordnance Survey map of 1854 we see that the church stood close to its eastern edge, several miles away from the other borders. Hoylandswaine township, which lay within the neighbouring parish of Silkstone, included Cat Hill, Well House and High Lee and stretched right down to the River Don at Nether Mill opposite Water Hall and at Boulder Bridge, Spring Vale. The shape of Penistone parish suggests that it was carved out of the enormous territory that was once served by Silkstone Church, which included Barnsley, Cawthorne, Dodworth, Stainborough, Thurgoland and detached parts of Cumberworth and West Bretton. It seems possible that the original Silkstone parish covered the whole of the sub-division of the West Riding that was known since Viking times as Staincross wapentake. But Penistone had become an independent parish by the 1120s at the latest, when the tithes and other dues of Silkstone were granted to the monks of St John the Evangelist at Pontefract.[1]

The exact size of Penistone parish was hard to determine before

The forty townships of Staincross wapentake. Penistone parish comprised the eight most westerly townships.

the moors were enclosed and accurate surveying techniques were employed by the Ordnance Survey, but by Victorian times it was accepted as covering 22,773 acres.[2] In common with the neighbouring parishes that stretched over the Pennine moors, it had to be divided into townships for local government purposes. In the north of England these townships were the basic unit of government from before the Norman Conquest until the creation of urban and rural district councils in 1894. Penistone parish was divided into eight townships, six of which were also recorded as small manors in *Domesday Book* (1086). These divisions were clearly of some antiquity and they still have some meaning today. The townships varied considerably in size, depending on how much moorland they contained. Gunthwaite (952 acres) and Langsett (4,914 acres) were not mentioned in *Domesday Book*, but Denby (2,865 acres), Hunshelf (2,465 acres), Ingbirchworth (1,105 acres), Penistone (1,134 acres) and Thurlstone (8,116 acres) were named, as were Oxspring and Roughbirchworth, which afterwards ceased to be a separate manor and became absorbed in Oxspring township (1,202 acres). We shall look at each of these townships and manors in detail in chapter 3.

Alric, or Ailric, was the Lord of Penistone and many other West Riding manors before and after the Norman Conquest. He was unusual amongst Anglo-Saxon landowners in retaining his estates under Ilbert de Laci, the Norman lord of Pontefract Castle. One of his privileges was the advowson of Penistone, the right to present rectors, which passed to his son, Swein, and his grandson, Adam, before it was split between Adam's two daughters. Penistone had two rectors until 1233, when the Archbishop of York insisted on just one. Successive lords of the manor presented rectors until 1358, when the right of advowson was given to the college of St Stephen in the Palace of Westminster.[3] This college had been founded ten years earlier by King Edward III and until its dissolution in 1547 it was housed in a famous Gothic building. The tithes (a tenth of each person's earnings) and other rights and dues of two out of every three South Yorkshire churches were granted to religious institutions during the Middle Ages, so this gift was not unusual. In fact, St Stephen's also received the tithes and advowson of Wakefield and Kirkburton churches. The dean and college of St Stephen did not take full advantage of their rights at Penistone until 1413, when they became rectors and appointed a vicar to serve in their place. The minister of Penistone Church has been a vicar since that time. As was usual, the college gathered the 'great tithes' of Penistone parish and the vicar was given the remaining third. In 1549, two years after the college

Penistone Church, a view taken by Joshua Biltcliffe after the restoration of 1904, before the trees were fully grown.

was dissolved, the Crown sold the right to present vicars to the Bosvilles of Gunthwaite Hall and the tithes to the Earl of Shrewsbury at Sheffield Castle. Since 1915 the Bishop of Wakefield has presented vicars. When Gilbert, the seventh Earl of Shrewsbury, made his will in 1616 he gave the tithes of Penistone to the Shrewsbury Hospital that he founded for the elderly poor of Sheffield.[4] The trustees of the hospital still pay the vicar £16 per annum and the association with Penistone is preserved in the name of Shrewsbury Road, a new road of the nineteenth century that descends the hill on the south side of the church, and by Talbot Road, for that was the family's surname.

St John the Baptist's Church

The parish church is by far the oldest building in Penistone. When it was completed in the late Middle Ages it would have appeared even more dominant than it does now, for all the domestic houses in the parish were timber-framed. The dedication to St John the Baptist seems to be the original one, for it was recorded in the Archbishop of York's register in 1232.[5] As we shall see, part of that early church is recognisable within the present structure. Churches are rarely an architectural unity because sufficient resources were not usually available to rebuild in one campaign and because the nave was the responsibility of the parishioners and the chancel that of the rectors, while chantry chapels were sometimes added by wealthy individuals. The scrappy documentary evidence from the Middle Ages is insufficient for precise dating of the various architectural features of Penistone Church, so comparative methods based on styles have to be used to unravel the story of the building.

The dignified tower at the west end of the church is of the Perpendicular style of Gothic architecture, the supreme period for English church towers, from the middle of the fourteenth century until the Reformation two hundred years later. Penistone's tower is similar in style to that at Silkstone, which was completed in 1495, and to those at Darton and Royston, which are carved with the marks of the Silkstone masons. The tower of Wentworth old church can be dated to about 1497 by the will of John Skiers, that at Almondbury to 1486 by an indulgence granted that year to all contributors.[6] This was clearly the time for rebuilding church towers in south-west Yorkshire. William Wordsworth, the long-serving Vicar of Penistone, died in 1495; perhaps the building of a new tower to match those of neighbouring parishes was a scheme launched by a younger, enthusiastic successor. If we date the tower to about 1500 we shall not be far out. Eighty feet high, carrying eight bells, and adorned originally by eight pinnacles (two of which were placed in the churchyard during the 1904 restoration), Penistone church tower is all of one build and is decorated with a series of worn grotesques under the battlements and by floral patterns carved around the west door. No evidence of a previous tower survives.

From the outside the nave and its aisles look to be of the same period as the tower. Responsibility for these parts of the church lay with all the inhabitants of the parish, whether from private donations or from collective efforts at fund raising such as church ales. The battlements and pinnacles on the roof line and the mullioned windows in the aisles and the clerestory are all in the late-medieval style that we call Perpendicular Gothic. But the south doorway to the nave is in an earlier style of about 1300 and as it is in its original position the adjoining walls of the aisles must be older than their external stylistic features suggest. The Perpendicular windows of the aisles must therefore have replaced earlier ones. When we go inside the church, the warm, natural colour of the millstone grit walls provides an unexpected contrast with the blackened exterior. The nave and the aisles are built in rows of even masonry right up to roof level, so perhaps the clerestory windows, too, replaced earlier openings? Once we are inside the nave, it is evident that the church

The interior of Penistone Church is much older than the exterior. This view down the nave into the chancel shows late twelfth and thirteenth century work.

is much earlier than the date suggested by its external appearance. The style of the alternate circular and octagonal piers which divide the nave into six bays is of the late-Norman period of about 1200, three hundred years earlier than the tower. If the nave arcade was built about 1200, the aisles must also have existed then, but they were probably remodelled a hundred years later, judging by the south door, the chancel arch and the arches at the east end of the aisles, all of which date from about 1300.

When churches were re-designed, part of the old structure was often kept in place to support the adjacent walls during rebuilding. The walls were then plastered and no-one could distinguish the old from the new until the Victorians stripped the plaster to expose the bare masonry. At the eastern end of the north aisle the northern wall of the chancel arch now has some walling that was never meant to be shown. Part of the masonry is arranged in a herringbone pattern that can be dated to the eleventh century. Below it, another part of the wall can be identified as a piece of an Anglo-Saxon cross shaft that the early Norman builders re-used as common building stone. These tiny remnants take the history of the church back to about a thousand years ago.

The nave roof is one of the glories of the church and it dates from the re-designing of the nave and the building of the tower about 1500. The designs of its thirty-three bosses and twelve timber corbels are open to different interpretations, for we have no firm evidence. The head of St John the Baptist on a charger is carved above the chancel arch, with Tudor roses on either side. The man and woman in the nearest corbels may perhaps represent the Baptist's parents. Clues are provided by heraldic devices such as that of the Archbishop of York and two *fleur-de-lys* pointing to royal patronage through Penistone's membership of the Duchy of Lancaster. Henry VII was monarch at the time. The other carvings have naturalistic patterns, such as grapes and acorns. The medieval stained glass has all gone, but in 1629 Roger Dodsworth, the Yorkshire antiquary, noted that the arms of the Turtons of Smallshaw and Millhouse, the Oxsprings and Robert Pilley, the vicar who died in 1459, were still displayed in the chancel.[7] The present glass dates from the long ministry of Canon W S Turnbull, who was vicar from 1855 to his death in 1913.

Even to the untutored eye, the chancel is seen to have been built in a different style from the nave. The dean and college of St Stephen's, Westminster, did not match the efforts of the parishioners in re-designing their part of the church. The chancel has no Perpendicular battlements or pinnacles to mark the roof line and the windows are in the style known as Early English Gothic. Two pairs of carved clerics' heads can be seen high on the eastern wall, representing perhaps members of St Stephen's college. From the churchyard we can readily see that the walls of the chancel have been heightened above the south window, where the top part is inscribed with the date 1691, and we can observe the original pointed roof line that is marked on the external eastern wall of the nave. From within the chancel and the Lady Chapel we can see where different masonry

Penistone Church from the south-east. The chancel was the responsibility of the dean and college of St Stephen's, Westminster, the tower and nave that of the parishioners, and the Lady Chapel that of private individuals.

distinguishes the heightened roof line from the section below. The stonework beneath the great east window and in the north wall of the chancel is also different from that above. If we go inside the vestry, a straight joint where the north wall of the chancel was extended to the east is revealed. This joint proves that the original Norman chancel was a short, rectangular structure, a bit narrower than the nave.

The Norman chancel seems to have been extended to its present length about 1300, judging by the style of its south and east windows which have intersected tracery of the Early English or Decorated periods. The weathered heads at the bottom of the south window surround depict a man with a hair style of 1250-1350 and a woman with a wimple that had gone out of fashion by about 1330. The great east window is basically that which was inserted about 1300, when the walls were raised to accommodate it, but a late nineteenth century photograph shows that it once had six (not five) lights. The priest's door is also in the Early English style, though the small window above it is later. The original Norman chancel was extended about the same time as the walls of the nave aisles were rebuilt and a new south door formed the public entrance to the church.

To summarise, we have a little evidence for an eleventh century church, the nave and the chancel were built about 1200, the nave aisles were refashioned and the chancel was enlarged about 1300, and the nave was modernised and a sturdy tower was built about 1500. We have still to consider the two chantry chapels that were attached to each side of the chancel and which were once served by their own priests. The present Lady Chapel was founded by the fourteenth century, when Roger de Gunthwaite bequeathed 6d per annum to the service of the Blessed Virgin Mary and the same sum to the maintenance of a light before the great crucifix and Adam Russell gave

8d and a silver candlestick to 'stand before the statue of the Blessed Virgin Mary in her chapel within the church of Penistone'.[8] The documentary evidence is supported by that of the architecture, for the mouldings of the arches leading into the chapel are similar to those of the chancel arch that we have dated to about 1300 and the east window of the Lady Chapel is in the same Early English style as the window on the south side of the chancel. St Mary's Chapel or the Lady Chapel is mentioned in several other wills that were made between 1450 and the dissolution of chantry chapels in 1547.

This grotesque head once supported the arch that led from the north aisle to the nave into the chantry chapel of St Erasmus and St Anthony.

During this final phase the chapel was restyled with a Perpendicular south window that was raised up to a new roof.

The chapel on the north side of the chancel was dedicated to St Erasmus and St Anthony. The arch leading from the north aisle of the nave has been removed but the grotesque head that acted as a corbel to support it has been left in place. In 1529 William Marshall, a Denby yeoman, left a bequest to the chantry priest of St Erasmus within the parish church of Penistone 'to sing and celebrate mass and other dyvyn service att the awter of Seynt Hearsme'. In 1629 Roger Dodsworth noted that this chapel had been rebuilt by William and Johanne Wordsworth about 1530 in honour of Saints Erasmus and Anthony and that William Benson was the chaplain who served it.[9] The wall of the north aisle of the nave continues in a straight line along the chapel, which was given a matching Perpendicular window with a slightly-raised roofline. The south aisle is the more splendid of the two, for it has an extra window and better-quality masonry.

In the Middle Ages the interior of the church had a very different appearance from now. The walls were plastered white and probably bore paintings of Biblical scenes and the lives of the saints. A rood screen with the images of the crucified Christ, the Virgin Mary and St John the Evangelist divided the nave from the chancel and images of Our Lady and Saints Erasmus and Anthony were the focal points of devotion in the chantry chapels. At the Reformation the images were taken down, the paintings removed and the chantry chapels dissolved. Behind the chancel arch we can see the holes where the rood screen was once fixed to the wall. The northern chantry chapel eventually housed the organ. In 1542 Richard Wattes, the vicar, had bequeathed 'a pare of organs to the Churche of Penniston' and 'a plainge book for the organs'.[10] The first substantial organ was bought by public subscription in 1768.

The interior of the church became the final resting place of the better-off parishioners. In the eighteenth and nineteenth centuries their memorials were fixed to the chancel walls. The most intriguing is that of William Fenton of Underbank, who was 'murderously slain by robbers in Algeciras', and the most splendid is that of Godfrey and Bridget Bosville of Gunthwaite Hall. Their marriage in 1681 is also commemorated in an armorial achievement painted by Henry Gyles of York, the most famous glass painter of his age, that was brought from the hall and re-fixed in a clerestorey window in the nave. The rest of the parishioners were buried in the churchyard, where the tombstones date from the late seventeenth century to the opening of the Stottercliffe cemetery in 1880.[11] Their inscriptions remain remarkably clear because of the quality of the local stone, but even in the nineteenth century, most people were buried in unmarked graves.

The churchwardens accounts tell of routine maintenance work over the years but of no further major alterations until Victorian times.[12] The clock which was fitted to the church tower in 1817 to replace the old scratch dial on the buttress to the south of the door immediately became one of the most valued and memorable features of the town centre. In 1862, under the leadership of Canon W S Turnbull, Penistone entered into the spirit of the times by re-designing the church interior. The box pews were replaced by free seats, the musicians were removed from the west gallery, the pulpit was taken down from the fourth pier from the west and replaced by a new one and a lectern, choir stalls were placed in the chancel, the great east window was given new painted glass, the walls were stripped bare and the north door of the nave was blocked up. Meanwhile, the churchyard was given new walls and Shrewsbury Road was constructed to provide an alternative route to the ancient one down Church Hill.

St John's Chapel

The porch leading into Penistone Church was built in the eighteenth century with stones from St John's Chapel in Chapel Lane. Two medieval grave covers were used as seats and holy water stoups found a new use. The purpose of the old chapel is uncertain, though many another medieval parish had such a building standing alone in the fields beyond the settlement. Some were founded alongside holy wells. Ecclesfield had its St Michael's Chapel and Barnburgh had one dedicated to St Ellen. Each gave their name to a communal townfield divided into strips. They all seem to have been regarded as chantry chapels and so were dissolved by Edward VI's government in 1547, like the chantry chapels that were attached to churches.

The first reference to the Penistone chapel is in an undated charter of the thirteenth century, when John, the son of William de Peniston, granted land to Elias Baldwin del Rode, including a piece lying to the west of the chapel of St John. In 1439 one of the parties to a charter was John del Rodes, the custodian of the chapel of St John at or near Penistone.[13] The custodian seems to have lived by the chapel as a hermit. In 1630, long after the dissolution of the chapel, a survey, valuation and rental of lands belonging to Penistone Grammar School included

> *The Hermit Yard containing by estimation three Roods, and lying on the South side the highway leading up from the Chappell, and abutting on the Scyte of the said Chappel late called St John's Chapel.*[14]

At the dissolution of the College of St Stephen the chapel seems to

The tower and south aisle of the church, with the porch that was built in the eighteenth century with stones from the former chapel of St John.

have been part of their possessions, for in 1560 a lease of the former lands of the college to Thomas Burdett and William Hawkesworth required the tenants to repair the late chapel of St John the Baptist and all houses, barns and tenements belonging to it.[15] In 1697 the vicar, Edmund Hough, wrote,

> *This chapel, though built of very meane stone, is yet extraordinarily well cemented together... It is now for the most part demolished, the walls thereof having been since my coming to be vicar taken to repair the churchyard walls.*[16]

The site was cleared about 1771. A survey and map of 'Land lying at Old Chapel', made by Phineas Wordsworth of Schole Hill in that year[17] identifies the site of the chapel with the last house on the left of Chapel Lane before the farm known as New Chapel. The footpath that leads towards the top of Clarel Street was marked on the map as 'The Lane-Road to Chapel Field', one of the two open fields of Penistone. The twenty-seven acres attached to this property may have originally formed the endowment of the priest, or 'custodian', of this medieval chapel which stood in the countryside to the south of Penistone for nearly three hundred years.

Chapter Three

Lords of the Manor

✠

After the Norman Conquest the whole of Penistone parish formed the south-western part of the great lordship that was known as the Honour of Pontefract and which later in the Middle Ages became absorbed into the Duchy of Lancaster. Like other feudal magnates, the De Lacis of Pontefract Castle granted manors within their honour to their followers in return for military service when called upon. These manors had belonged to Anglo-Saxon or Viking lords before the Conquest. One of the few lords to hold on to his possessions after 1066 was Alric (or Ailric), a great landowner within and beyond the Penistone district who was succeeded by his son, Swein, and his grandson, Adam FitzSwein, before the male line failed. Hoylandswaine probably took its name from Alric's son to distinguish it from High Hoyland and Upper and Nether Hoyland.

Penistone

One of the daughters of Adam FitzSwein granted the manor of Penistone to a clerk named John de Penigston. The surname, which was spelt in a variety of forms, became hereditary and several charters of the De Peniston family survive up to 1306, when Cecilia, the daughter of another John de Peniston, granted the manor to William Clarel of Aldwark, knight, the descendant of John Clarel, warden of the chapel of Tickhill Castle, a prominent clergyman and royal courtier.[1] The Clarels were absentee lords of Penistone until 1489 and their successors, the Fitzwilliams and Foljambes, also lived in gentry residences in other distant parts of South Yorkshire. Once the De Peniston family disappeared, the manor house was let to tenants.

No records of the meetings of the courts of this manor survive, but other evidence proves that part of the old manor was granted to the dean and college of St Stephen's, Westminster, when they acquired the advowson and tithes of Penistone parish. The college held their own manorial courts at Penistone from at least 1486 until their dissolution in 1547, when the rights were bought by the Bosvilles of Gunthwaite. The Bosvilles continued to hold meetings of their 'court baron of the Manor of Penistone' until at least 1794, in order to register transfers of land.[2]

Water Hall, the seventeenth century home of the Wordsworth family, alongside the old track across the River Don to Gunthwaite. Wentworth Road is in the foreground. A housing estate now dominates this view.

The manor house of the De Penistons seems to have been on the site now occupied by the seventeenth and eighteenth century building known as Water Hall. An undated medieval deed records a grant of land by 'William ad Aquam lord of Penistona' and another grant of about 1300 was made by 'John ad Aquam of Peniston'.[3] These Latin forms translate as 'at the water'. Water Hall is in an unusual position, close to the River Don, at the northern edge of Penistone; perhaps it was moated in the Middle Ages before the present stone building replaced a timber-framed one? The absence of a corn mill within the manor of Penistone is perplexing, for a mill was normally a prized possession which the tenants of the manor had to use, but Nether Mill, which lay on the other side of the Don, just within the manor of Thurlstone, may have fulfilled this role, for it was an ancient possession of the Wordsworths of Water Hall.[4]

In the eighteenth century the Wordsworths became lords of the (original) manor of Penistone, but by then this title did not mean much.[5] Where the Wordsworths came from is a puzzle that might be solved by the new technique of DNA analysis of the Y-chromosome (which is passed from father to son) in a sample of men bearing the same and similar surnames. By the late fifteenth century the family name was sometimes written and pronounced Wadsworth, but this may have been because of confusion with a separate name, which originated at Wadsworth, near Halifax, and which became widespread in West Yorkshire.[6] The earliest spellings of the name that became Wordsworth suggest that Wardleworth, across the Pennines near Rochdale, was the more likely source. Nicholas de Wordulworth was recorded at Penistone in 1408 and William Wordelsworth was there in 1441.[7] The Wordsworths had not arrived in Penistone by 1379, when the poll tax returns recorded a Richard and Alice 'atte Waterhall', but perhaps they knew the Turtons, who were taxed in Thurlstone township at that time and who came from the place of that name a few miles to the west of Wardleworth?[8] The poll tax returns for Penistone also name William and Joan Proctour, whose daughter, Elizabeth, was to marry Nicholas de Wordulworth. William Proctour's ancestor, Thomas le Procuratour, was recorded in Penistone in 1306;[9] a pocurator was an attorney in a spiritual court. Two centuries later, the Wordsworths traced their family tree back to this marriage and recorded it in an unusual manner. Rydal House in the Lake District, once the home of the poet, William Wordsworth, has an inscribed oak chest which was made in the year 1525 at the expense of William Wordsworth, son of William, son of John, son of Nicholas, husband of Elizabeth, daughter and heir of William Proctour of Penistone. In 1536 this chest was referred to as 'a great arke' in the will of William Wordsworth of Penistone, the founder of the chantry chapel of St Anthony and St Erasmus.[10]

The Wordsworths became a prolific family in and near the parish of Penistone. A younger son, William Wordsworth, became chaplain of the Lady Chapel, then Vicar of Penistone from 1459 to 1495. By the reign of Henry VIII the Wordsworths had branches at Water Hall, Snowden Hill, and just beyond the parish at Lower Falthwaite, Stainborough (the home of the poet's ancestors). During the sixteenth and seventeenth centuries other branches settled at Softley, Schole Hill, Gravels, Shepherd's Castle, Carlecoates, Thurlstone,

Brookhouse (Langsett) and Swaithe (Worsbrough). Ralph Wordsworth of Water Hall, gentleman (1591-1663) built the present Water Hall and the barn which has a 1641 datestone; his eldest son, John, moved to Swaithe, so his younger son, Josias, inherited Water Hall. Josias had four sons: John of Water Hall and Burton Grange (a Monk Bretton property which he acquired through marriage); Josias, a London merchant; Elias, a Sheffield mercer; and Samuel, another London merchant. The family's fortunes clearly improved dramatically during the seventeenth and eighteenth centuries as a result of their success in business. John's son, Josias, followed his uncles in making his fortune in London as a merchant trading with Sweden and Russia. His son and namesake (1719-80) was the Josias Wordsworth who led the subscription to build Penistone Cloth Hall in 1763 and who, upon his marriage to a daughter of a wealthy London merchant, built Wadworth Hall, near Doncaster, to the designs of the leading architect, James Paine. They had two daughters but no sons and so in 1825 Thomas Vernon Wentworth of Wentworth Castle, Stainborough, bought the manor of Penistone and Water Hall. The nearby Wentworth Road was named after him.[11]

The original manor of Penistone seems to have covered the same area as the local government unit known as the township, a total of 1,134 acres. The River Don formed its northern boundary, in the west Penistone was separated from Thurlstone by the Hen Brook and Coal Pit Dike, in the south Mossley Dike marked the boundary with Langsett township, and in the east Kirkwood Beck formed the boundary with Oxspring. Watercourses were commonly used as boundaries in the hilly terrain of the West Riding. Unusually, all the townships of Penistone parish seem to have been identical with small manors. These units were of great antiquity and all but Gunthwaite and Langsett were recorded in the *Domesday Book*. But Oxspring township combined two *Domesday Book* manors: those of Oxspring and Roughbirchworth.

Until its market was established in 1699, Penistone was just a hill-top village clustered around the church, with a High Street stretching southwards towards the village green and St Mary's Street descending the hill towards St Mary's Well, near Bridge End. As in all the small settlements on the edge of the Pennines, the best land was divided into strips in communal 'townfields' and all the everyday decisions about farming were taken in the manor court. The records of this court do not survive, but deeds speak of two large fields: East Field and Chapel Field.[12] Most Pennine townfields were re-arranged by the agreement of the farmers in the sixteenth, seventeenth and eighteenth centuries. At Midhope, for instance, just beyond Penistone parish, the townfields were enclosed in 1674.[13] Beyond the Penistone townfields lay the 'intakes' or clearings made by medieval farmers, such as Cubley, Hackings, Joan Royd, Lumb Royd and the group of labourers' cottages at the western edge of the township at Scholes. Stottercliffe takes its name from a stud-fold or enclosure for breeding horses.[14] The poorest land on the hills to the south was common grazing ground until it was enclosed in 1819-26, when the present rectangular fields and straight lanes were created. Race Common takes its name from the annual horse races that were held there in the eighteenth century.[15]

Oxspring

Alric's son, Swein, was lord of Oxspring and Roughbirchworth both before and after the Norman Conquest, so it was natural for the two manors to become united. By the thirteenth century the lord was a local man named De Oxspring. Richard de Oxspring and Matthew de Oxspring were recorded here during the reign of Henry III and junior branches of the family moved to other parts of South Yorkshire, where the surname became well established. In the second half of the fifteenth century the male line failed with William de Oxspring and the manors passed through marriage to the Eyre family for three generations until they were sold in 1547 to Godfrey Bosville of Gunthwaite Hall.[16]

The present village of Oxspring is not shown on Thomas Jeffreys's map of Yorkshire in 1772, but he marked the site of the former Manor House or Lodge on the opposite side of the River Don and that of what is now called High Oxspring alongside the top road from Thurgoland to Ingbirchworth. The Manor House occupied a commanding position on an outcrop of shale above the river by the original 'ox spring'. For centuries the manor of Oxspring consisted of just a few scattered farms and two mills. In, or shortly after, 1547 Godfrey Bosville erected the building that was described at the beginning of the twentieth century as 'The Lodge or Manor House'. It had certainly been completed by 1580 for in that year Bosville's will refers to the 'bed and bedsteads at my lodge at Oxspring, and tables and forms there, with all harness, cross-bows, rack and artillery'.[17] Bosville used it both as a hunting lodge and as the meeting place of the Oxspring manor court, but as he normally lived at Gunthwaite, the lodge was let to tenant farmers. It became uninhabitable in the late nineteenth century and fell into ruin during the decade before the First World War. Old photographs show that

Oxspring Lodge, shortly before its demolition in Edwardian times. It had been erected in the reign of Queen Elizabeth by Godfrey Bosville of Gunthwaite, half in timber, half in stone.

thick stone walls masked a timber-framed building in the post-and-truss style, which was about thirty-eight feet long, twenty-five feet wide and two-and-a-half storeys high. One room had oak panelling, but elsewhere the timbers were exposed and the gaps between them were filled with well-tempered clay. The staircase wound its way round a newel post with solid oak steps nine inches deep and twelve inches wide.[18]

Below the manor house stood the Oxspring manorial corn mill, the

Oxspring corn mill about the time of the First World War. A manorial corn mill occupied this site on the River Don from at least the thirteenth century.

last of the nine ancient mills on the Don as it flowed through Penistone parish. The long goit leading to the dam can be traced from Willow Bridge. A corn mill was recorded in the thirteenth century during the time when Matthew de Oxspring was lord and, according to a datestone, it was rebuilt in 1652. John Rolling, the first member of the family who worked this mill from about 1800 to 1915, bought it from the Bosvilles in 1830. Two years previously, he had built a steam corn mill alongside Barnsley Road; this was burnt down in 1856 and replaced by a new structure which has now gone.[19] The River Don was also the source of power for another mill in the Middle Ages, the lord's fulling mill or walk mill, where cloth was scoured and felted after it had been woven. In 1306 Robert de Oxspring had granted part of this mill to Henry de Rockley and further references appear in the records from the sixteenth century onwards. They include one in 1549 to the 'Walke mylne goit' and another in 1729 to 'Oxspring walk miln'.[20] In 1743 John Wood of Oxspring was one of three local fullers who agreed not to full the cloth of any clothier who did not use the new cloth market at Penistone, and the township had at least five clothiers in 1806.[21] The woollen trade disappeared from Oxspring later in the nineteenth century. Nineteenth century maps mark 'Walk Mill Bank' by the site that was occupied from 1888 by Winterbottom's wire mill, the successor to a wire works founded by Joseph William Wordsworth about 1862. The water wheel was dismantled about 1947.[22]

In Elizabethan times the River Don was used for another industrial venture, that of forging iron. The records are tantalisingly brief, but it is clear that the first Godfrey Bosville, lord of the manor of Oxspring, leased a site to George, the sixth Earl of Shrewsbury, who was applying new technology to his ironworks in and around Sheffield at that time. In 1575 the jury of the Oxspring manor court ordered John Wainwright 'to stop up his pond between Oxsprynge and le Smythes'. Nine years later, 277 blooms of iron were made at 'Oxspringe Smethies' and a letter written early in 1585 claimed that, 'For want of hay at Oxspring for the horses the Smithies there cannot work'.[23] Nothing more is heard of these ironworks and the site has not been identified.

The Oxspring manor court rolls of 1549 record the usual grievances and the jury's decisions. Various inhabitants were charged with taking in bits of the common, cutting down trees, breaking hedges, diverting a stream, digging stones, and fishing in the 'Walk Mill goit'.[24] The manor and township of Oxspring extended northwards over the hill towards Silkstone, as far as the Storrs Dike. South of the Don the township included the former manor of Roughbirchworth, so that altogether it covered 1,202 acres.

The two *Domesday Book* estates which were marked by birch trees became distinguished from each other as Roughbirchworth and Ingbirchworth ('ing' meaning meadow). The so-called Roughbirchworth Manor Farmhouse appears to have been a small, single-storey building of the mid-seventeenth century that was enlarged in Victorian times. The few farms of the hamlet are strung out along the lane and, remarkably, the pattern of the old field system as far west as the Kirkwood Beck is preserved by field walls which follow the long, narrow, slightly curving lines of the medieval strips. In 1618 parts of 'the common field of Roughbirchworth' were called the Overfield, the Ryefield, and the Longleyes.[25] Sometime in the next hundred years or so the farmers must have agreed to abandon communal farming under the direction of the jury of the manor court in favour of individual ownership, but instead of paying a surveyor to re-design the fields in rectangular shapes they built their walls along the old boundaries between the strips.

The medieval strip pattern of the townfields of Roughbirchworth is preserved by the stone walls that were built when the farmers abandoned communal agriculture in the seventeenth or eighteenth century. The rectangular fields date from the enclosure of the commons and wastes in the early nineteenth century.

A prehistoric earthwork known as Shepherd's Castle (which gave its name to Penistone's Castle Green) marked the boundary between Oxspring and Hunshelf townships where the common of Roughbirchworth met that of Snowden Hill. The earthwork was about 120 yards in diameter, but has been mostly ploughed out except on the western side. In 1818 a private *Act of Parliament* authorised the enclosure of the 250 or so acres of common land that lay on the southern edge of Oxspring township; the process was completed eight years later. Until the early nineteenth century it had been possible to walk all the way from Oxspring to Thurlstone over bleak moorland. A curious feature resulting from the enclosure award of 1826[26] is the narrow tongue of land that protrudes from Oxspring township towards Throstle Nest. No doubt this was designed to allow access to the Hartcliff-Green Moor road. Throstle Nest was known as Bleak Royd or Blake Royd in old boundary perambulations, where the township of Oxspring met those of Hunshelf and Langsett. The exact line of the boundary between Oxspring and Hunshelf had been disputed until agreement was reached in 1756. The agreed line went from Oxspring pinfold along

Dawson Mill Brook to three new boundary stones, one of which still stands prominently in the field near Tanyard Farm to the south of Roughbirchworth.[27] The brook fed Pearson's tan pits and the pond of Dawson's Mill, which was worked as a corn mill by the Dawson family in the seventeenth century and as the Camm family's wire mill in the eighteenth century before it was converted into a woollen mill in the 1830s by Joseph Booth. The dam survives alongside the ruined buildings.[28] Kirkwood Mill, on the western edge of the township, was once the only building between Penistone and Oxspring. It obtained its water from Castle Dam and Kirkwood Beck and in the eighteenth and early nineteenth centuries it too was a woollen mill.[29]

Hunshelf

The adjoining manor of Hunshelf was another of Alric's possessions when the *Domesday Book* was compiled. 'Hun's shelf' is a late Anglo-Saxon place-name for a flat piece of land on the ridge by Hunshelf Hall.[30] The present hall is an eighteenth and nineteenth century building, but it probably stands on the site of the medieval house of the De Hunshelf family, the local lords of the manor from at least the late thirteenth century. The date 1746 is marked in the pediment above the door. How long the De Hunshelfs continued there is not known, but their name eventually disappeared in South Yorkshire and by Elizabethan times the manor belonged to the Wortleys of Wortley Hall across the River Don.[31]

The manor and township of Hunshelf covered 2,465 acres of farm land, commons and wastes that sloped down Black Moor and Green Moor to the River Don in the north and the east and descended the steep Hunshelf Bank to the Little Don in the south. The rivers meet at Deepcar, the 'deep, marshy valley overgrown with brushwood'. By the late thirteenth century the De Hunshelfs had a manorial court mill on the Little Don, where, in the nineteenth century, Samuel Fox developed his steel works. Stocksbridge takes its name from a small bridge over the River Porter or Little Don that was erected by a member of the Stocks family, possibly the John Stocks who was recorded in 1716 and who had a fulling mill nearby.[32] Meanwhile, a series of iron forges, slitting mill, tin mill and wire works were sited on the left bank of the Don in Thurgoland and Wortley townships, just outside Penistone parish.

The medieval townfields of Hunshelf were still being farmed in strips on the best land in 1725.[33] The hamlet of Snowden Hill, known until the nineteenth century as Snodden Hill (the 'bare, bald hill'), also had townfields and its own common.[34] The hamlet consists of

The scattered settlements of Oxspring and Hunshelf townships are depicted on Thomas Jeffreys's map of Yorkshire 1772, a generation or so before the enclosure of the commons and wastes.

Broad
Cal

Head Hurst

SILKSTON

Gother Bottom

Roger Royd
Pye Grave

Noble Thorpe

Fell Lane

Cat Hill

Hoyland Swayne

Doe Well

West thorpe

Tinker House

Moor Side

Knab proper

High Royd

oter

Habbs Berry

Heely

Willy House

Hadley House

Wath Hill

Orspring

Coit Hill

Bower Hill

Hollin Dyke

DENISTON

Cubley

Rough Birchworth

A

High Fields

East

Dan H

Royd Fields

Black Moor

K

The

Bleak Royd

Dison Coite

14

Snowden Hill

Dean Head

Huthwaite

Sheep Ho.

Under Bank

12

Well Hill

Hunshelf

HOPE DALE

Hunshelf Bank

Windy Bank

Holly Hall

Langley Brook

Green

Stocks Bridge

Park

four farms and a scatter of small houses and it has changed little since the first edition of the Ordnance Survey six-inch map of 1854. Its buildings date mainly from the eighteenth and nineteenth centuries, but the cross-wing at the south end of the Cloth Hall retains a number of original features from the seventeenth century, including a six-light parlour window, and the hall block is dated 1723. The 1854 map marks Tenter Lane, another indicator of a former woollen cloth industry. Snowden Hill Mission was started at Chapel Farm in Victorian times by Canon Turnbull, Vicar of Penistone.

The sturdy timbers of the medieval barn at Dean Head, a fine survival from the Middle Ages.

The most interesting farmhouse in Hunshelf township is that at Dean Head, which has a hall block and a much altered cross-wing that dates from the late Middle Ages, though not as far back as 1379, when Johanna del Dene paid poll tax here. The medieval barn is much better preserved, though its aisles were removed when the whole building was remodelled in stone in the seventeenth century. It retains its original common rafter roof and was similar in style to the (demolished) barn at Shore Hall, Thurlstone. Other medieval sites below Hunshelf Bank include Avice Royd, Pea Royd and Briery Busk. Underbank Hall was built as a gentry residence for William Fenton in the middle of the eighteenth century, after his marriage to Frances, the heiress of four generations of the West family. It is marked prominently on Thomas Jeffreys's map of Yorkshire in 1772 and may have been erected on the site occupied by Peter Underedge in 1379. The enclosure of the commons and wastes of Hunshelf township between 1800 and 1813 produced the regular, geometric field patterns that are particularly evident on Black Moor and led to the building of new farm houses in the distinctive Pennine style of the first half of the nineteenth century.

Langsett and Penisale

When Godfrey Bosville of Gunthwaite Hall led the first attempts to found a market at Penistone in 1698 he claimed that the parishioners had long possessed the right to hold a weekly market and an annual fair under a charter that had been granted in 1290 to Elias de Midhope, Lord of the Manor of Penisale. His claim was rejected by the government on the grounds that the rights had lapsed and that, strictly speaking, they did not apply to Penistone, but it is interesting to find that in the late seventeenth century local people remembered the old market and fair, which had been founded four hundred years earlier but which had long since been discontinued. It is interesting, too, to find that they were familiar with the name Penisale, which by then had long since fallen out of use except as an alternative name of an old moorland manor. Perhaps Bosville had access to the original charter, or a copy, for he knew the exact days on which the market and fair had been held centuries earlier?

Local historians have long puzzled over the exact site of Penisale. The earliest references to the place date from 1190-1208, which is as early as one might reasonably expect records to survive for a manor that was not named in the *Domesday Book* of 1086 and which did not belong to Alric or Swein. In the earliest documents, Penisale was variously spelt Penigheshal, Penighalg, Peningsale, etc.[35] The first

element of the name is obviously the same as that in the name of
Penistone, which was recorded in the *Domesday Book* as Pengeston
and Pangeston, and in the late twelfth century as Peningeston. While
it is possible that this element was derived from an Anglo-Saxon
personal name, it is more likely to have come from the Celtic word
'pen', meaning a prominent hill, as in Pen-y-Ghent (Yorkshire) or
Pendle Hill (Lancashire). The second element, 'halgh', is another
which occurs elsewhere in England; it means a nook of land on the
edge of an estate. Both elements of the name help us in our attempt
to locate the site of the manor. Although Penisale appears under
various spellings in later charters, it is not listed in the various tax
returns – the poll taxes and lay subsidies – of the fourteenth century.
We may wonder therefore whether Penisale was not an actual village
but the name of a district. A parallel can be drawn with Ecclesall
(now a Sheffield suburb), which was not a settlement but a district
on the boundary of the estate served by the Celtic church at
Ecclesfield. Indeed, the various spellings of Penisale indicate that
the name was probably pronounced as if written '-sall', as in
Ecclesall. The 'pen' to which the name refers was perhaps the great
ridge which separates Penistone from Midhope and which ends in a
prominent head at Hartcliff. The 'tun', or central settlement where

*The township of Langsett, otherwise Penisale, shown on Thomas Jeffreys's map
of Yorkshire (1772).*

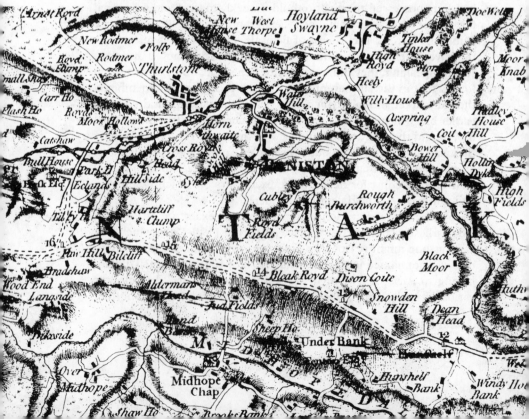

the parish church was built, lay on the northern side of this ridge; Penisale lay at the southern side, close to the parish boundary formed by the Little Don. But we cannot be certain about such matters. A less-likely possibility is the commonly-held view that the 'pen' was the hill that rises above the River Don and on which Penistone is built.

The approximate location of Penisale was known to the later inhabitants of the parish of Penistone. Legends grew up about its disappearance. John Ness Dransfield, who wrote a long-winded history of the parish in 1906, quoted a tradition that an old yew tree in the grounds of *Alderman's Head*, near the river, had been the site of the court of the manor of Penisale and the focal point of the market and fair, and he printed the text of a poem, *The Yew Tree of Penisale,* which had been written anonymously.[36] John Wilson, the eighteenth century antiquary of Broomhead Hall, had measured this notable yew and had found it to be twenty-five feet in circumference. Wilson recorded in his notebook that the tree had been set on fire by a Bradfield man in 1758 and that it had burnt for five days.[37] According to Joseph Kenworthy, the historian of Stocksbridge and Midhope, the yew tree was said to have stood in a field on the north side of the road from Stocksbridge to Langsett. Kenworthy discovered the foundations of buildings on the opposite side of the road, on the bank of the river, where oral tradition pointed to the site of an old corn mill.[38] It is worth noting that this valley road was not there when Penisale had a market and fair; the route was created in 1805 as part of the new Wadsley-Langsett turnpike road. The old highway from east to west followed the top of the ridge, high above the valley. The tradition of the yew tree is a dubious one that can neither be proved nor disproved, but the site seems too far from the highway to be a credible choice for a market place.

We need to return to the surviving documentary records in order to establish the extent of the manor of Penisale. Amongst the medieval sources are some references to the possessions of the monks of Kirkstead Abbey, a Cistercian house in Lincolnshire. These date back to at least the late twelfth century when William, the son of John, lord of Peningeston, granted land to the Kirkstead monks and his 'right in the moor next to their grange of Peningeshalg'.[39] The site of this grange, from which the lay brothers of the monastery farmed this moorland estate, is not known, but perhaps the name of Sheephouse Farm points to a likely candidate. When the abbey was dissolved in the 1530s it was said to have possessions in Penynghall, Midhope and Langsett.[40]

Langsett is the name of the moorland township that covered 4,914 acres in the south-western part of Penistone parish. The name is now confined to the small village by the reservoir that was constructed in 1904 at the edge of the moors, but it was once applied to the whole township, which stretched up and over the hillside to the north of the Little Don. The earliest spellings show that the name was originally Langside, the 'long side' of the great ridge or pen which had probably given its name to Penisale. Langside or Langsett seems, in fact, to have been an alternative name for Penisale. This was certainly the case by 1818, when the 'Manor of Langsett alias Penisale' was offered for sale. In 1871 the *Dog and Partridge* public house was the scene of the meeting of the 'Great Court Baron of Sir Lionel Melbourne-Swinnerton Pilkington, baronet, Lord of the Manor of Pennyshall otherwise Peningesale (sometimes called Langside or Langsett)'. In 1890 particulars of the owners and occupiers within the manor show that properties there extended throughout the township of Langsett, from Sheephouse in the east to Swinden in the west.[41]

The district known as Penisale therefore seems to have been identical with that otherwise called the township of Langside or Langsett. In 1290 the Lord of the Manor of Penisale, Elias de Midhope, obtained two royal charters, one allowing him to hunt throughout his manor, the other to hold a market each Tuesday and an annual fair on the eve, day, and morrow of the feast of St Barnabas, that is 10-12 June. In 1307 the next lord of the manor, William de Sheffield, took the precaution of obtaining new charters to confirm these rights.[42] These charters of 1290 and 1307 are the only pieces of documentary evidence that we possess concerning the holding of markets and fairs at Penisale, though, as we have seen, the memory of these open-air marts on the edge of the moors was long preserved by oral tradition. Elias de Midhope was following the example of numerous other lords who founded markets and fairs in thirteenth and early fourteenth century England, at a time when the population was expanding and commercial opportunities were promising. Many of these enterprises were soon abandoned, however, for the Black Death of 1348-50 and other pestilences reduced the national population considerably and trade contracted severely. Hooton Pagnell, Braithwell, Wortley and Wath-upon-Dearne were amongst other South Yorkshire villages which lost their markets and fairs during the late Middle Ages. Penisale's experience falls into a wider pattern of initiatives that were unsustainable during a long period of recession.

The seventeenth century range at Alderman's Head, built on a dramatic spur overlooking the Little Don valley.

The farms within Langsett township which are on sites that were occupied in the Middle Ages include Belle Clive and the ruined hall at Swinden. The most spectacular position is that of Alderman's Head, on a promontory high on the north side of the valley of the Little Don. The part of the farmhouse that dates back to the seventeenth century has been restored, after having been burnt out in the 1930s. Both the site and the name suggest an old establishment, but the earliest reference to the place is from 1581.[43] Alderman is not a local surname, nor is there any evidence that a man of the status of an alderman (perhaps of Doncaster or York) once lived here, though this seems the likeliest explanation of what remains an unanswerable puzzle. Many other farms within the township were created after the enclosure of the commons and wastes in 1811-14.

Thurlstone

At 8,116 acres Thurlstone was by far the largest manor and township in Penistone parish, stretching westwards over the moors beyond Dunford Bridge to Saltersbrook and to a disputed moorland boundary with Holmfirth. Although it formed part of the great

The first edition of the six-inch Ordnance Survey map of Thurlstone (1854) shows the regular plan of the old part of the village and Top o' th' Town, the possible site of the original farmstead.

An aerial view of the stone walls that fossilise the medieval strip pattern in Thurlstone's West Field.

Honour of Pontefract, Thurlstone was not granted to local lords, as were the neighbouring manors, but to the absentee Savilles of Elland and later of Thornhill, a powerful West Riding gentry family who had originated in Normandy and whose South Yorkshire possessions included Saville Hall, near Dodworth, and the manor of Tankersley. They are commemorated locally by the name of Saville House, a farmstead near Hazlehead.

Thurlstone's name is a combination of the Anglo-Saxon tun and the Old Danish personal name, Thurulf.[44] Clearly, the Vikings had taken over an existing settlement and had re-named it after their local lord. Comparisons with other settlements in different parts of the country suggest that the farmhouse known as 'Top o' th' Town', set high on a spur, may well have been the original settlement before the present village was planned on the level ground below at some unknown date before or after the Norman Conquest.[45] Travellers along the busy Manchester Road do not see the old village, high above the river valley. They pass only the nineteenth century buildings that were erected near Plumpton Mill and so get a false impression of Thurlstone's history. The 1854 Ordnance Survey six-inch map shows that old Thurlstone had a regular plan, with the crofts and tofts of the former farm houses in Town Gate stretching back to shared boundary lines, some of which can still be followed on the ground. Judging by our knowledge of many other Yorkshire villages, this planning dates from either the late Anglo-Saxon and Viking era or from the time of the Normans, but we have no documentary evidence to confirm this suggestion. The planning included the creation of two open fields to the west and east of the village. These communal fields survived until 1696, when they were enclosed by the agreement of the twenty-six farmers who owned strips.[46] The narrow, curving pattern of these strips is preserved by some of the walls within the former West Field (whose name survives in Westfield Farm and Westfield Avenue), but the enclosers of the East Field created a new pattern of closes on either side of Long Lane. Other, smaller townfields were once farmed within Thurlstone township at Carlecoates and Ecklands.[47]

The old village contains many seventeenth and eighteenth century houses in typical West Riding styles, some of them with early nineteenth century rows of weavers' windows inserted in their chambers or in an extension. A good example of a seventeenth century house with later windows stands at the beginning of Royd Moor Road; a later house with a row of ten windows is tucked away near Providence Chapel. Thurlstone township lay at the heart of the farming and hand-loom weaving district within Penistone parish. Old photographs show that Towngate, the central street, was narrower than it is now, with three-storeyed buildings rising at either side. It is a matter of regret that several of the most distinctive buildings have been demolished, including a three-storeyed house by *The Crystal Palace* which had a row of fifteen weavers' windows under the eaves and another range of windows on the middle floor.[48] Another farmhouse which has gone is Smithy Fold, opposite Towngate Farm, the birthplace of Penistone parish's most famous son, Dr Nicholas Saunderson (1682-1739), Lucasian Professor of Mathematics at Cambridge University, Fellow of the Royal Society and the only local person to appear in *The Dictionary of National Biography*. Blinded by smallpox as a child, he astonished university audiences by lecturing on optics. He was educated at Penistone Grammar School and at the Nonconformist Academy at Attercliffe before going on to Cambridge.[49] His tombstone lies behind the high altar at St

Dr Nicholas Saunderson (1682-1739), Lucasian Professor of Mathematics, educated at Penistone Grammar School.

Peter's Church, Boxworth, a few miles from Cambridge.

Beyond the village are several farmsteads with old buildings on medieval sites. Smallshaw was rebuilt in 1664, Royd Moor Farm has a 1693 datestone and Bank House Farm was built in 1727. The sturdy timbers of the demolished Shore Hall barn, on the northern 'shore' of the Don, were erected in the late fifteenth century. Hornthwaite's cruck barn was erected right at the end of the timber-framed tradition in 1759;[50] its name means 'boar clearing'[51] and it goes back to Viking times, like Gunthwaite, Linthwaite and Slaithwaite further north, or Huthwaite in Thurgoland township. Ecklands was recorded in the thirteenth and fourteenth centuries in various guises, such as Eckelholes. By the second half of the sixteenth century the name had changed to Ecland and Eckloynes and by 1647 to Eclans. The first element is derived from Viking speech and seems to be either the Old Norse personal name Ekkill or a word denoting

This seventeenth century house at the beginning of Royd Moor Road was given a range of weavers' windows early in the nineteenth century.

Shore Hall barn (now demolished) had sturdy medieval roof trusses, similar in style to those at Dean Head.

Maythorn Cross. This photograph was taken at New Mill just a few days before it was removed to its approximate position in the Middle Ages, on the boundary between Thurlstone township and the Graveship of Holme.

poor, unproductive land.[52] High on the moors to the west, the Savilles had a vaccary, or cattle-rearing farm, at Windleden, the 'windswept hill overlooking a valley', that was recorded in the early fourteenth century and marked prominently on a map of about 1600.[53]

No less than 6,522 of Thurlstone manor and township's 8,116 acres were classified as commons and wastes before their enclosure in 1812-16. Streams acted as natural boundaries wherever possible, but elsewhere crosses had to be erected. The Maythorn Cross on Whitley Common was recorded in 1435 and shown on an earlier fifteenth century map of the Graveship of Holme;[54] its exact positioning remains a matter of dispute between the inhabitants of Holmfirth and those of the western parts of Thurlstone township to this day. The boundary line has long been hotly contested. Back in 1274 complaints were heard that Earl Warenne of the manor of Wakefield (which included Holmfirth) had extended his hunting area well inside Thurlstone township.[55] This simmering dispute erupted in the reign of Henry VIII in a violent feud between Sir Henry Saville and Sir Richard Tempest. In 1524 the Court of Star Chamber heard a complaint from Saville that Holmfirth men, 'having recently taken in their own common', were driving their cattle on to Thurlstone's commons. Thurlstone farmers had taken turns to keep watch and to drive the cattle away, but when it was Robert Moxon's turn he was attacked by Richard Furness and Thomas and John Beever of Holmfirth, who dragged him by the arm and knocked him to the ground, threw him into the river and almost kicked him to death. Edward Marsden saw what was happening and came to help, but he was overpowered and taken with Moxon to the bailiff's house in

Holmfirth and then to Sandal Castle. Many Thurlstoners went to seek justice at Sandal, where they found Moxon had died. Sir Richard Tempest refused to have the case judged at the scene of the crime, but agreed to a trial at York Assizes.[56] The Thurlstoners returned home, whereupon Tempest passed a 'Not Guilty' verdict. We do not know the outcome of this case, but it shows to what violent lengths men went to protect what they thought were their rights and how difficult it was to agree on boundaries before accurate maps were drawn in the nineteenth century.

The style of the language in the earliest recorded perambulation of Thurlstone's boundaries[57] suggests that it was made in the fifteenth century. Entitled *The Lymytts and Bounds of the Lordshyp of Thyrlston* it reads:

> *Begynnyng at Denbebrygge, and so by the heghweye to Heynbroke, and so frome seyd Heynbrok to Brokhows, and so from sayd Brokhous to the Greyhoundstone, and so frome sayd Greyhound Stone to Hertclyff Cros, and so frome sayd Herclyffe Crosse by the heyghweye to the Ladye Crosse, and so from sayd Ladye Crosse by the welle unto the Salterbroke, and so by the sayd Salterbrok to the hed of the sayd brok, and so from the hed of the sayd Salterbroke, by the ded hegge, unto Snaylsden, and so by the heyght of the sayd Snaylsden unto the Styeweye in Harden, and so from the sayd Styewey in Harden unto the Horre Lawe, and so frome sayd Horys Lawe, as streyght as kane by lyned to the Marre thorne, and so frome sayd Marye thorne to the Standing stone, and from sayd Standand ston to the Brodstone, and frome the sayd Brodstone to Byrchworth Ledzatt, and so frome sayd Byrchworth Ledzatt, downe by Meyrysbroke, to the watter of Done, so by sayd watter of Done to the sayd Denbye bryge, and wher sayd bounder dos begen.*

These boundary points agree with those recorded on a map made about 1600 for the Savilles and a plan and notes made two hundred years later, when boundaries were being disputed prior to parliamentary enclosure.[58] Together, they enable us to trace the old boundary of Thurlstone township on the map and the ground. Denby Bridge, the usual starting place for perambulations, is now known as Bridge End. The boundary followed the road alongside the Don as far as the Henbrook, a small stream whose valley rises towards Sike House (the 'boundary steam' known as Brook House in the earliest perambulation). But when the boundary turned west up the hill over former moorland towards Hartcliff, its line had to be marked by crosses and here our problems begin. Was the medieval

48

This medieval boundary cross stands in a field next to the road from Penistone to Hartcliff. It marked the boundary between the townships of Thurlstone and Penistone and may be the one marked as 'New Cross' on a map of c.1600.

cross shaft and base that stands in a field near Cross Lane the New Cross that was marked on the map of c.1600, but not named in the perambulations? If so, why was the Greyhound Stone marked before the New Cross, when its present position (approximately that recorded on the 1854 Ordnance Survey six-inch map before it was built into the wall of the drive to Bella Vista) is much further west? The Greyhound Stone is recorded in the fifteenth century perambulation, but the present stone is nowhere near as old as that. It appears to be a replacement of about 1800. It is inscribed 'MWB' or 'MWP' and is similar in style to stones

The Greyhound Stone has been moved at least twice and is an eighteenth century replacement of the one named in a fifteenth century perambulation.

erected on the Hoylandswaine-Cawthorne boundary about the same time for William Bosville of Gunthwaite. An alternative suggestion is that the inscription refers to the manor of William Payne of Langsett. This William Payne, it was claimed in the notes accompanying the perambulation of about 1800, had destroyed and buried another cross that had stood by the roadside at Hartcliff.

The Thurlstone-Langsett boundary then followed the road down the hill to Fullshaw Cross (where another old boundary stone has disappeared) and on to Boardhill and the original course of the highway to Lady's Cross and Saltersbrook, the county boundary. Lady's Cross was recorded in the thirteenth century, when it marked the limit of grazing land that was granted by the lord of Glossop to Basingwerk Abbey (Wales).[59] Here again, boundaries were disputed; despite the cross, the Manor of Glossop did not extend beyond Saltersbrook into Penistone parish. The Thurlstone boundary went up the brook as far as the boundary with the Graveship of Holme (the old name for the Holmfirth district), and then turned north-east along a line marked by stones, ridges and the old track by which salt was taken to Wakefield market. The 1600 map marks Salters' Gate going from Upper Nab, past Maythorn Cross to Birds Nest, and along the present minor road through Victoria. The boundary then turned southwards towards the Mearsbrook ('boundary brook') and the Scout Dyke ('overhanging cliff or bank') as far as its confluence with the River Don at Nether Mill, close to the starting point at Bridge End.[60]

Bullhouse corn mill at the beginning of the twentieth century. An earlier mill belonging to the Rich family ground corn here in 1486.

Thurlstone manor and township contained most of the old mills of Penistone parish. The River Don has provided water-power for scores of mills, iron works and grinding wheels on its long course through Sheffield, Rotherham and Doncaster towards its confluence with the Humber. Bullhouse Corn Mill was the first mill downstream from the source of the river. It was already working by 1486 when the Rich family came to Bullhouse and it remained part of the estate that was attached to the hall until 1904, when it was sold (with a farm of forty-six acres) to the existing tenant, Benjamin Goldthorpe of Catshaw Farm. An overshot wheel with a drop of 11½ feet was fed by a large, wedge-shaped pond, now filled in but once a calm and lovely backwater. Both my grandfather and my uncle worked as waggoners at the four-storey mill. In the 1920s it specialised in grinding animal 'feeding stuffs of every description, all of the best quality'. The family firm also acted as agents for Silcock's and other famous names, providing 'linseed and cotton cakes' and different types of meal and flour. In the 1940s the Goldthorpes advertised their business as that of 'Corn Millers and Cake Merchants' who made pig, cattle, poultry and chick foods and fertilisers.[61] The water-wheel ended its days in 1963 after I had left Catshaw. I had not been aware that I was witnessing the end of an era that had lasted half a millennium.

Just beyond the mill a weir led water from the river into a long channel, or 'goit', to a second mill that was originally used for fulling cloth and was later converted for the production of wire. This was the mill which gave Millhouse its name. It belonged to the Rich family in 1598. A deed of 1627 refers to a property 'called Mylnehouse and the fulling mill adjoining with the dam, etc.'. The insertion of an 'n' into the name was typical of northern speech. Thomas Jeffreys's map of Yorkshire in 1772 marks the house and the mill but shows no other buildings nearby on Millhouse Green, a small piece of common grazing land. The six-inch Ordnance Survey map of 1854 marks the Fulling Mill and the adjacent Mill House, with a row of tenters for stretching and drying cloth after the fulling process was completed. Scribbling machines for preparing yarn had probably already been added, but in 1865 William Smith of Thurgoland converted it to the manufacture of wire. The mill was burnt down in 1926.[62]

Another goit or mill race fed a third mill downstream. This started life in the eighteenth century as a paper mill. The 1854 map names it the Old Paper Mill, for by then it was at least a century old. In 1876 it was converted into an umbrella works by William Hoyland.[63] Three more mills stood on the banks of the Don at Thurlstone. The first was another fulling mill, recorded as such in 1598 and known later as

An aerial view of Bullhouse and Millhouse about 1966. Three mills were powered by the River Don, including the one that gave its name to Millhouse.

Batty Mill, after Edward Batty, a clothier who died in 1661. It was still known as Batty Mill in 1813, when it was used for fulling and scribbling, but soon it became the Plumpton Cloth Mill, the property of the Tomasson family of Plumpton Lodge.[64] Downstream stood the Thurlstone or Hornthwaite Corn Mill, which had been worked since at least 1308.[65] This mill was partly demolished in 1959 to reduce the dangerous bend in the road and the remaining part of the building was converted into a house in 1970. Just beyond Thurlstone, an Oil Mill was erected on a new site in 1740 by James and John Walton to crush linseed. A case brought by Aymor Rich in 1764 claimed that his corn mill at Thurlstone was fed by an ancient goit, 124 yards long, and worked by two water wheels, one of which was very ancient. In the summer of 1761 the corn mill had been rebuilt and given a new wheel, which did the work of three old ones. His complaint was that the weir of the Oil Mill had obstructed the course of the river so much that a bed of wreck, just above the weir, stretched forty yards up the river and was ninety yards in circumference, so that the water re-flowed up to his tail goit to within thirty yards of his new water wheel, which he could not work.[66] The

Nether Mill, when it was owned by W H Hinchliff & Sons. It stood at the eastern edge of Thurlstone township and was fed by goits from the Scout Dyke and the River Don.

Oil Mill building was later converted to a cloth mill and then to a variety of other uses, but the site is still recognisable as that of the old mill. Finally, at the eastern end of Thurlstone township, we come to the Nether Corn Mill, or the Copster Mill as it was known in 1652. A deed of 1711 refers to

> *that water Corne Mill commonly called or knowne by the name of Nether Mill alias Copster Mill.*

At first, it was fed by a goit coming from the Scout Dike and a lease from Thomas Wordsworth in 1615 referred to it as the 'water corn mill called the Skoute', but in 1687 the Grammer family from Bakewell took over the mill and in 1721 Mary Grammer bought land to 'make a new cut or channel from the Don to Copster Mill Damm'. Two years later, another deed speaks of the dam and the water corn mill 'lately erected by the said Mary Grammer'.[67] The goit from the Don can still be traced across the fields.

Denby

The largest township in the northern part of Penistone parish was that of Denby, which covered 2,865 acres. The place-name means the 'farmstead of the Danes', which suggests that Danish settlers were relatively thin on the ground in this predominantly Anglo-Saxon district. The *Domesday Book* entry is unusual in mentioning a vaccary, or cattle-rearing farm, at this early date. Alric held the manor from the De Lacis of Pontefract Castle, but by the second half of the twelfth century the local lords had taken the name of De Denby. In 1304 the estate, including the manor of High Hoyland, passed through the marriage of Idonea de Denby to Robert, the younger son of Aymor Burdett. The Burdetts were a junior branch of a family from Rabodanges in the *département* of Orne, Normandy; Hugo Burdett was a landowner in Leicestershire at the time of the *Domesday Book*, but no firm descent can be proved.[68] Nicholas Burdett had the status of franklin, just below that of gentleman, when he paid poll tax at Denby in 1379. At that time, he was the richest man in Penistone parish, but he was much lower down the social scale than the knights of neighbouring parishes. The Burdetts lived at Denby Hall for twelve generations until they sold the manor to Sir William Saville of Thornhill, who also owned the adjoining manor of Thurlstone. In 1719 John Warburton's map of Yorkshire notes that Denby Hall was owned by Sir George Saville, though it would have been occupied by tenants. It stands in a prominent but isolated position, well to the east of the hamlets of Upper and Lower Denby, and seems to contain no traces of medieval work. Junior branches of the Burdetts stayed in other parts of Denby after the main line left; indeed, six separate households were recorded in the hearth tax returns of 1672.[69]

The townships of Denby, Ingbirchworth and Gunthwaite, shown on Thomas Jeffreys's map of Yorkshire (1772).

The present Ordnance Survey map still marks the former townfield to the west of Lower Denby, where land was once farmed in strips, but the characteristic fields in this northern part of the parish were the irregular-shaped royds and stubbings that had been cleared from the woods in the Middle Ages to create farms such as Denroyd, Dobroyd and Moor Royd. Settlements were small and scattered at Nether End, High Flatts, Birds Edge, Bagden and Denby Dyke. The extensive Denby Common lay immediately to the west of Upper Denby and stretched as far as the boundaries of Shepley, Cumberworth, Ingbirchworth, Thurlstone and the Graveship of Holme. The prehistoric earthwork known as Castle Hill, where stone axes from Westmorland and other Neolithic material have been found, acted as a boundary point in the west. The River Dearne was the old parish boundary to the north and streams such as the Broadstone Dyke acted as other divisions, but a dispute of 1566 between Denby and Gunthwaite shows that where no natural features were available the boundaries were marked by an 'old casten dyche' or 'great border trees'.[70]

In 1772 Thomas Jeffreys's map of Yorkshire marked the manorial corn mill amongst the cluster of houses known as Denby Dyke and a fulling mill downstream, which was known by the puzzling name of Putting Mill. They had probably once belonged to Richard Burdett of Denby and High Hoyland, who in 1545 had a water mill and two fulling mills on the River Dearne (the other one being at Scissett).[71] In the late eighteenth and early nineteenth centuries many more textile mills were erected on the banks of this river and Denby Dyke became known as Denby Dale.

The medieval lords of Denby were the only ones to build their own chapel-of-ease because of the distance of their residence from Penistone Church. William de Denby built this chapel between 1229 and 1232, but we know of it only from its foundation charter. It had long fallen out of use by 1627, when 'the inhabitants of Denby and Gunthwaite' petitioned the Archbishop of York 'that they were two or three miles distant from their Parish Church of Peniston, and that in winter time it was often with the greatest difficulty, and even with danger of death, that they were able to resort to it, in consequence of the overflowing of the waters'. The chapel that they erected was replaced by the present church in 1842. Probably all three buildings were on the same site at Upper Denby.[72] In the seventeenth century the prevailing religious spirit in Penistone parish was that of puritanism, but the Blackburn family were resolute Roman Catholics. Stewards of the Duke of Norfolk and builders of the

Bolsterstone glass house, they were of gentry status and at various times they lived at Hunshelf Hall, Alderman's Head and Lower Denby, where their house is still known as Papist Hall.

Ingbirchworth

Ingbirchworth was another of Alric's manors at the time of the *Domesday Book*, but nothing is heard about a manor in later times. The Reverend Joseph Hunter's conclusion was that Ingbirchworth 'seems never to have been more than a few farms cultivated by a race of yeomanry'. From the fourteenth to the late seventeenth century the leading family were the Micklethwaites, who took their name from 'a great clearing' between Silkstone and Cawthorne that is now known as Banks Hall. A large number of original features survive in the farmhouse and barn that John Micklethwaite built in Ingbirchworth in 1624. It is still the most striking house in the village. The senior line of the family died out with John's elder son, but a younger branch continued with Elias, a merchant who was a Member of Parliament and twice Lord Mayor of York and whose son settled at Swine, in Holderness.[73] The Micklethwaites who still live in the district are descended from other junior branches.

The spaces between some of the old farms at Ingbirchworth have gradually been built up so that the settlement has fused into a street village. Other old farms, such as Annot Royd (a clearing named after a woman), stand alone in a township that extends over 1,105 acres. Green Farm and Willow Farm are seventeenth century structures

The house erected by John Micklethwaite in Ingbirchworth in 1624. An original window survives in the gable to the left, but the others have been replaced.

and Ingfield Farm has a cruck barn. Most of the farmers were also
clothiers and were dependent upon their grazing rights over the
commons and wastes until these were enclosed in 1800-13.

Gunthwaite

Gunthwaite was the smallest township in Penistone parish at 952 acres
but it was the home of the most important family, the Bosvilles.
'Gunhild's clearing' was derived from an Old Norse feminine name, so
it must go back before the Norman Conquest despite its absence from
the *Domesday Book*. After the Conquest it was an independent manor
that belonged to Alric and which by the late thirteenth century had
become the home of the De Gunthwaites. The manorial water corn
mill that was mentioned in documents of 1348 and 1360 and which
was worked until 1956 occupied the site in the valley below the hall
where the dam survives. Much of the land in the township belonged to
the lords of the manor, but a small estate at Broad Oak, which was
originally called the Rodes, was granted to the Knights Hospitaller.[74]

In 1374 the manor of Gunthwaite passed to Thomas de Bosville of
Ardsley, who had married the heiress, Alice de Gunthwaite. Seven
years later, Thomas acquired a grant of free warren and created a deer
park to the south of the hall. The Bosvilles came from Normandy and
were one of the most important and enduring of the knightly families
of South Yorkshire. They took their name from Beuzeville-la-Giffard,
a small place near Dieppe which today consists of a church and a few
farms, some of them timber-framed. The first recorded Bosville in
South Yorkshire was Elias de Bosville, who in the middle decades of
the twelfth century lived at Harthill, close to the Derbyshire border.
He was a leading follower of the De Warennes of Conisbrough Castle,
who hailed from Varenne, not far from Beuzeville.

After the marriage of Sir John Bosville to Alice, the daughter and
heiress of Hugh de Darfield, in the early thirteenth century, the
Bosvilles' main residence in South Yorkshire was at a fortified manor
house between Ardsley and Darfield, known originally as New Hall
but now Cranford Hall. The Bosvilles lived there for about four
hundred years, while junior branches were established at nearby
Middlewood Hall, Braithwell, Chevet, Conisbrough, Ravenfield,
Warmsworth and Wickersley.

Gunthwaite was not a major residence of the Bosvilles until the
middle of the sixteenth century. About 1460 the Gunthwaite estate
was settled on a younger son, whose chief residence was at Beighton.
His descendant, Godfrey Bosville (c.1517-80), was the first of the
family to live at Gunthwaite for much of the time, but even he styled

Gunthwaite barn. This substantial barn measures 163 feet in length and 44 feet in width. Divided into eleven bays by sturdy king-post frames, it has three waggon entrances. It was erected in the mid-sixteenth century for Godfrey Bosville and is still a working barn.

himself in his will as 'of Beighton, esquire'. He had married Jane, the sister of Bess of Hardwick, and had built a timber-framed house at Gunthwaite which was demolished in the nineteenth century after it caught fire. The mid-sixteenth century hunting lodge which he erected half in timber half in stone at Oxspring has also gone, but his famous barn at Gunthwaite remains intact as one of the glories of Penistone parish.

Other buildings at Gunthwaite date from the late seventeenth century, from the time of the third Godfrey Bosville ('Justice Bosville') and his wife, Bridget Hotham, a member of a prominent East Riding gentry family. The summer house in the garden is inscribed 'GBB 1688' and the elaborately designed stable block is carved 'GBB 1690'. Godfrey became Lord of the Manor of Midhope in 1690 and rebuilt the chapel there when he was High Sheriff of Yorkshire in 1705. Upon his death in 1714, he was succeeded by his nephew, William, then by William's son, Godfrey Bosville the fourth. This last Godfrey moved to a modern house at Thorpe in the East Riding upon his marriage and the connection with Penistone parish was weakened. His estates passed through marriage to the MacDonalds of the Isles, which is why Portree on the Isle of Skye has a *Bosville Hotel* in Bosville Street.[75] By the later years of the eighteenth century, the families which had been the most important in Penistone parish since medieval times had all died out in the main line.

Chapter Four

Farming Families

✠

Medieval farms

Many of the halls and farmsteads in the ancient parish of Penistone are on sites that were occupied in the Middle Ages. Although the medieval timber-framed farmhouses have been replaced by stone buildings, some of the barns are still supported by sturdy wooden posts or by pairs of oak crucks that date from the fifteenth, sixteenth or seventeenth centuries. As we have seen, the best land that surrounded the villages and hamlets was once farmed communally in 'townfields', which were divided into strips for the growing of cereals, but these were gradually enclosed by the agreement of the local farmers between the sixteenth and eighteenth centuries. Beyond the communal fields lay the various medieval 'intakes', which in this part of the West Riding were often known as 'royds'. These irregular-shaped fields had been cleared laboriously from the

Alderman's Head cruck-framed barn, a type that was commonly used in the fifteenth, sixteenth and seventeenth centuries by farmers in the Penistone district and neighbouring parishes.

Upper and Lower Belle Clive farms. The site has been occupied since at least the early 1200s. It gave rise to the local surname Bilcliff or Biltcliffe.

woods and wastes between about 1150 and 1350 for use as separate closes, pastures and meadows. Documents of about 1300, for instance, refer to Malynrode (in Penistone) and Jonrode (just beyond Penistone's western border in Thurlstone), two intakes that were named after the men who had cleared them.[1] These names have disappeared but those of Lumroyd and Joan Royd survive nearby. About forty 'royd' names have been recorded in Penistone parish, but only a minority became attached to farms; most were simply field names. Beyond these intakes the extensive common pastures and moors stretched to the township boundaries.

It is rarely possible to date the foundation of the medieval farms that were created beyond the villages and hamlets. The *Domesday Book* names the manors that existed at the time of the Norman Conquest, but no other local documents survive before the thirteenth century. Some farms may have been old when they were first recorded. Belle Clive, for example, first appears in a document that can be dated between 1208 and 1211,[2] but the farm may have been created long before in the Anglo-Saxon period. The original name was 'Billa's cliff', an appropriate description of a farm perched high on the hillside. It gave rise to the local surname Bilcliff or Biltcliffe, the name of Penistone's photographers, Joshua and his son, John Thomas. It did not assume its present form of Belle Clive until the first edition of the six-inch Ordnance Survey map of 1854. My mother lived at Upper Belle Clive as a child and always pronounced it Bilcliff or 'Billcley'. The change from Snodden Hill to Snowden Hill also dates from the time of the first Ordnance Survey six-inch map. The surveyors from the south of England did not always catch what the locals said to them.

Some of the farms in the outlying parts took their names from wild animals that had roamed in the area, such as the cats of Catshaw, the deer of Hartcliff and the badgers of Brockholes. For centuries, these animals were regarded as pests that should be exterminated. The surviving churchwardens' accounts for 1696-1703 record payments to local people who had killed numerous 'foomards' (polecats), martens, foxes and badgers and a 'mart', which might have been a weasel or a ferret rather than a marten.[3]

The clearing of new land in the Middle Ages did not proceed in a smooth, uninterrupted way, but in fits and starts and with many reversals. A series of bad harvests, cattle plagues and sheep murrains between 1315 and 1322 caused considerable hardship throughout the land. As a result of these catastrophes, the amount of tax paid by the inhabitants of Penistone parish fell from £53 6s 8d in 1291 to £20 in 1341.[4] The returns of another national tax known as the lay subsidy of 1334[5] note the amount paid by each of the eight townships of Penistone parish. The tax was levied at a time when nearly every family earned their living from farming and when Penistone was just a small village clustered around the parish church. The amount of tax paid gives an indication of the number of farms in each of the townships: Thurlstone £2 16s 0d, Langsett £1 3s 0d, Hunshelf £1 1s 0d, Denby £1 0s 0d, Oxspring 16s 0d, Penistone 14s 0d, Gunthwaite 13s 4d, and Ingbirchworth 7s 0d.

Two generations later, the poll tax returns of 1379 provide a similar ranking. This tax was levied on everybody over the age of sixteen, though at lower rates than in 1334. Thurlstone township again paid most with 16s 10d, followed by Denby 11s 8d, Hunshelf 9s 10d, Langsett 9s 0d, Penistone 5s 2d, Gunthwaite 4s 6d, Oxspring 4s 2d, and Ingbirchworth 3s 2d. Langsett and Oxspring had slipped down this order since 1334, but we cannot tell whether the Black Death and other pestilences had had any effect. A slightly different ranking is obtained from the number of people who were recorded in each township – Thurlstone: 56, Hunshelf: 44, Denby: 39, Langsett: 36, Oxspring: 18, Penistone: 18, Gunthwaite: 15, Ingbirchworth: 11. Both tax returns provide clear evidence that the village of Penistone was a small place before it obtained its market in 1699. It contained only 18 of the 237 tax payers in the parish.

The origins of some local surnames
The poll tax returns of 1379 are our first major source of information about local surnames, which were then in the process of becoming

Ranah Stones Cote. Now restored, this farmhouse has a 1784 datestone. The surname Reaney was derived from the site in the fourteenth century.

fixed and hereditary. Many of the most distinctive ones were derived from the names of farms. The surname Reaney, for instance, was pronounced Raney, for it was derived from Ranah Stones Cote, the 'ravens' mound' near Hazlehead. The present farmhouse dates from 1784, but it stands on a medieval site where Thomas de Ranaw paid 4d poll tax in 1379. By the seventeenth century the Reaneys had moved to Darfield and Sheffield. Half a mile to the east of Ranah Stones Cote, the local pronunciation of Bullhouse produced the surname Bullus. Some of the Bulluses had already moved to Sheffield by 1379, but a local branch must have stayed, for in 1413 John Bulhous was recorded as clearing new land in Thurlstone township.[6] The Appleyards were at Bullhouse before the Riches and they continued to live in Thurlstone township until the nineteenth century. They gave their name to Appleyard Wood, east of Ecklands, but the surname has another source further north in the West Riding township of Allerton, from where it became widespread. The Stainrods were another family who took their name from their farm. The Robert de Stenrode who paid 4d poll tax in Thurlstone township in 1379, and who had witnessed a deed at Carlecoates seven years previously, was descended from the inhabitants of a clearing known as Stevenrode, just across the boundary in Hepworth. The Stainrods later moved to Shelley and by the seventeenth century one branch had emigrated to New England.[7]

The poll tax returns for Thurlstone township also name three members of the prominent Turton family, whose ancestors had moved into south-west Yorkshire from the place of that name near Bolton in Lancashire. By 1379 a Ronksley had left Ronksley Farm

Swinden Hall. Now demolished, this substantial farmhouse was built for John Haigh in 1641.

on the Derbyshire bank of the River Derwent (by the present Howden reservoir) to settle here and a Swinden had moved from Swinden Farm on the edge of the moors in Langsett township, though a senior branch had stayed there. Thurlstone and Bakewell were the only two homes of people with the surname Drabble, a distinctive Peak District name that was derived from an Old English personal name or a nickname. Penistone township had a John de Bilclyf and a John Eclus from Ecklands. The Micklethwaites were already settled at Ingbirchworth and Roger Bosville, a mercer who was taxed 12d, headed the list at Gunthwaite, but the richest man in Penistone at that time was Nicholas Burdett, a franklin who headed the list in Denby township with a contribution of 40d, ten times the basic rate (a franklin was a substantial freeholder below the rank of gentleman). The surnames Denby, Hunshelf and Oxspring all appeared in the returns and Langsett township included William de Hatyrslay, a mercer taxed 12d, who had moved across the Pennines from Hattersley by 1367.[8] By the reign of Queen Elizabeth branches of this family had moved to Sheffield and other parts of south-west Yorkshire.

Penistone parish names in the late seventeenth century
During the reign of Charles II the government's main source of revenue was a tax levied on the fireplaces of every house except those of the poor. The best surviving return for the West Riding is that of Ladyday [25 March] 1672.[9] The names of 266 householders were recorded for Penistone parish, though unfortunately the exempted

poor were not listed. In other towns and villages the number of exempt often amounted to a third or more of the total householders. This then is not a complete record, but it is invaluable for providing names and for giving an indication of each family's social status through the number of fireplaces that they possessed. Well over half the population made do with just one heated room.

Gunthwaite Hall had twelve hearths, Denby Hall had nine, Water Hall and Hunshelf Hall each had seven, and Bullhouse Hall and Thomas Clayton's house at Denby had six. Another fifty-six householders were moderately well-off with three to five hearths, a further fifty-four paid for two hearths, and the remaining 150 were taxed on just one hearth each. If the exempted poor had been listed, the number of houses with a single hearth would have been greatly increased. This sort of social pyramid, tapering to a few gentry families, was entirely typical of England at that time.

When we look at the returns for the separate townships, some interesting contrasts emerge. At one extreme, Gunthwaite had just six households, only one of which had a single hearth. At the other, no-one in Langsett had more than four hearths and thirty-one householders paid tax on a single chimney.

Table 4:1
The hearth tax returns of Ladyday, 1672, arranged by township

Township	One Hearth	Two Hearths	Three Hearths	Four Hearths	Five Hearths	Six+ Hearths	Total Hearths
Denby	27	8	9	2	5	2[6+9]	53
Gunthwaite	1	3	1	0	0	1[12]	6
Hunshelf	19	13	2	3	1	1[7]	39
Ingbirchworth	2	4	1	4	1	0	12
Langsett	31	4	5	2	0	0	42
Oxspring	16	4	2	1	0	0	23
Penistone	10	9	2	2	2	1[7]	26
Thurlstone	44	9	8	1	2	1[6]	65
Total	150	54	30	15	11	6	266

These returns provide us with a list of surnames halfway between the period of surname formation and the present day. The Wordsworths, Riches, Micklethwaites and Burdetts were prominent, with numerous branches, and the locally-derived names Appleyard, Bullas and Swinden were still there. The most striking feature of the list, however, is the large number of names that had migrated south

from their original homes in the Graveship of Holme, the parish of
Kirkburton, the Huddersfield district and the Calder valley. The
Marsdens were by far the most numerous of these immigrants, with
fourteen households, followed by the Haighs with eight and the
Hinchcliffes with five. Others include Armitage, Beever, Broadhead,
Brooksbank, Coldwell, Dyson, Earnshaw, Firth, Helliwell, Horsfall,
Linley, Marsh, Matthewman, Milnes, Moorhouse, Roebuck, Senior
and Woodhead. Names from other parts of Yorkshire include
Dringhouse, Gawber and Shillitoe, but it is noticeable that few
families ventured north from Sheffield. The local Hampshires derive
their name from Hallamshire and perhaps the Thicketts came from
the same district. The Hawkesworths may have originated in the
Chapelry of Bradfield, but another source of the name is from
Halifax parish. The general drift of the population was clearly from
north to south. Even the few Peak District, Cheshire and Lancashire
names – Alsop, Armfield, Ashworth, Bagshaw, Baumforth, Brammah
and Charlesworth - may sometimes have arrived in Penistone parish
via Holmfirth and Kirkburton.

Another list of names is that of the men of Penistone parish who
petitioned for the establishment of a market in 1699.[10] As it has never
been printed before, it is reproduced here.

Table 4:2
**Petition in support of establishing a market in Penistone,
24 August 1699**

Adde, Thomas	Bray, Timothy	Coldwell, Josias
Apleyard, William	Broadhead, Joseph	Cooke, Jonas
Archer, Joseph	Brook, Joseph	Cooke, Jonathan
Askom, Robert	Brooksbank, Arthur	Couldwell, John
Bacon, Tho.	Brooksbank, Joshua	Couldwell, Joseph
Bagley, Joseph	Browksbanck, Joshua	Couldwell, William
Barber, Benjamin	Burdett, Amos	Couldwell, William
Barber, John	Burdett, Samll.	Crowder, William
Bartholomew, Peter	Burdett, Thomas	Denton, Dan.
Batty, Francis	Burdett, Thoams, Jun.	Denton, John
Batty, John	Burdett, Phillip	Dickenson, Henry
Beamont, James	Burgiis, Francis	Dickinson, Daved
Bentley, Samuel	Burgon, Francis	Dickinson, Edward
Blackburn, Ben.	Burgon, William	Dickinson, Elihu
Blackburne, Joseph	Chappell, Jonas	Dickinson, Henry
Blackburne, Robert	Charelsworth, Thomas	Dicson, Joseph
Blye, Nicholas	Charlesworth, James	Dongworth, John
Bower, Jonathan	Charlesworth, Joseph	Dongworth, John
Bramald, Charles	Chatterton, Jonathan	Dongworth, Thomas
Bramall, Edward	Claiton, Samuel	Earnshaw, John
Bramhall, Tho.	Clayton, Benjamin	Earnshaw, Meg(?)or the
Bray, Thomas	Cockin, Sam.	Earnshaw, William

Ellis, George
Ellies, Robert
Ellis, John
Ellis, John
Ellisson, Francis
Engille, Brice
Firth, Jeremiah
Frith, Simeon
Gaunt, Joshua
Gaunt, Tho.
Gibines [?], Christ.
Goddard, Joel
Godderd, Richard
Grant, George
Greaves, John
Greaves, John
Green, John
Green, Joshua
Haigh, Abraham
Haigh, Francis
Haigh, John
Haigh, Joseph
Haigh, Thomas
Haigh, Thomas
Haigh, Thomas
Hall, John
Hanwell, John
Hanwell, Richard
Harison, Timothy
Hawkesworth, John
Hawkesworth, Josias
Hawkesworth, Richard
Hawksworth, Richard
Heeley, Thomas
Hinchclyffe, Henry
Hobson, Thomas
Hoiland, Elias
Holinworth, George
Horsefield, Ab.
Horsefield, John
Horne, Henry
Hough, Edm. Vic[ar]
Hurst, George
Ibotson, Edward
Ingom, Jonas
Jessop, Joseph
Jessope, John
Kennerly, Josias
Kennerly, Richard
Kilner, James
Kilner, John
Lee, Matthew
Lindley, Tho.
Linley, Peter
Linley, Thomas
Marsden, Dan.

Marsden, Elias
Marsden, Henrery
Marsden, Josias
Marsden, Richard
Marsden, Will.
Marshall, Anthony
Marshall, Francis
Marshall, Jo.
Marshall, Richard
Mattiman, Fran.
Mellor, John
Michell, Joseph
Michell, Thomas
Mickelthwait, John
Mickelthwait, William
Mickelthwaite, Josias
Mickelthwaite, Richard
Micklelthwait, Richard
Micklethwait, John
Micklethwaite, Elyas
Milles, John
Millns, Emor
Mitchel, Abraham
Mitchel, John
Mitchel, John
Mitchell, Samuel
Morehous, George
Morton, Samuel
Morton, Tho.
Mosley, Joseph
Norris, William, of
  Denby, Cur[ate]
Norton, Samuel
Pasley, John
Pashley, Mich.
Pearkin, Ralf
Poole, Walter
Preist, William
Priest, John
Priest, John
Priest, John
Pytt, Edward
Ramsay, Jno.
Ramsden, John
Ramsden, Richard
Rich, Abel
Rich, Daniel
Rich, El.
Rich, Emor
Rich, John
Rich, Jonas
Rigley, George
Roads, Rogger
Robinson, Thomas
Robinson, William
Roebuck, John

Roebucke, Thomas
Rooebottom, Daniel
Russell, Valentine
Sanderson, Joseph
Saunderson, Josias
Senior, Thomas
Senior, Thomas
Shaw, John
Shaw, John
Shaw, John
Shaw, Jonathan
Shaw, Nathaniel
Silverwood, Joshua
Skelton, Joseph
Smalbent, Richard
Smith, Tobias
Staniforth, Nathan
Stocks [?], John
Street, John
Street, Valinntine
Swift, George
Swift, John
Swift, Jonathan
Swift, Josias
Talowbut, George
Thicket, John
Trout, John
Wainewright, George
Wainwright, John
Walker, George
Walker, John
Walker, John
Wallton, James
Walton, Edward
West, Francis
West, John
West, Rich., Capt[ain]
West, Stephen
Wilkinson, George
Wilkinson, John
Wille, Heanery
Wood, Francis
Woodcock, Elias
Woodkirk, Jonas
Woolley, James
Wordsworth, Gregory
Wordsworth, Isaac
Wordsworth, John
Wordsworth, John
Wordsworth, John
Wordsworth, Jonathan
Wordsworth, Matthew
Wordsworth, William
Wordsworth, William

Farming inventories

The inventories of personal estate that were attached to wills from the 1690s to the middle years of the eighteenth century provide rare details of the livestock, crops and equipment on the farms of the Penistone district.[11] One of the earliest is that of John West 'of Snodden Hill, yeoman', drawn up by his neighbours on 9 July 1696. West's farmhouse consisted of a living room, known in the Yorkshire fashion as 'the house', two parlours and a kitchen, with chambers above, one of which contained a small store of wool, wheels for spinning wool and linen, and some barley. Most of his capital was invested in his animals, which comprised six oxen, five cows, eight young beasts, a gray colt, fifteen sheep and nine lambs. His equipment included two wheeled vehicles known as wains, two ploughs, a pair of ox harrows and a pair of horse harrows, forks, spades, yokes, ropes, gears, saddles and a scythe. His lime and manure were valued at £6 and the grass and corn on the ground at £36. As a yeoman he was one of the better-off farmers in the parish.

An aerial view of Snowden Hill, a hamlet that still retains its old character.

When John Micklethwaite of Ingbirchworth died in June the following year, his farm equipment was valued at £9 1s 4d. and fifteen load of shilling [chaff] was thought to be worth £12 12s 0d. The appraisers then recorded

> *5 cows 4 oxen £35, 6 steers 2 heifers 3 stirks 3 calves £29, 1 horse 2 pack sadles £4, 99 sheep £27 10s 0d, seed and ploughing £6 10s 0d.*

Steers were young, castrated oxen and stirks were young bullocks or heiffers less than two years old. In February 1698 another yeoman, Thomas Roper of Bridge, in Hunshelf township, had hay and straw worth £3 and corn valued at £10 10s 0d in his barns. His livestock were appraised as

> *4 Cows £12, 4 Bullocks £12, 1 Heifer 1 Bullocke 3 Calves £7, 1 Mare £2 10s 0d.*

and his manure at 5s 0d. This inventory was taken in winter time, when his stock was low. Another one from the same season was that drawn up on 1 January 1698 for Ralph Marsden of Roughbirchworth, yeoman. His buildings consisted of an upper and nether house, an upper and little parlour, each with chambers above, a stable, a wainhouse and barns. After valuing his farm equipment at £11 16s 4d, his neighbours listed

> *1 horse 1 mare 2 sadles, etc. £8 2s 0d, Barns: Oates and Hay £57 10s 0d, Barly, 20 stone of Wooll, £16 10s 0d, 6 Oxen £30, 2 Stears £7, 6 Cows £19 10s 0d, 2 Heifers £5 5s 0d, 1 Bullock 1 Heifer 2 Stearks 4 Calves Swine £13, 155 Old Sheep £50, 60 Hog Sheep £12.*

Hogs were young sheep that had not yet been shorn.

The inventory of the personal estate of Thomas Morton of Langsett, yeoman, was taken on 29 October 1703. After visiting his dwelling house and parlour, the appraisers climbed upstairs to the great chamber, where they found

> *Cloth and fustion £3 14s 0d, Wooll £14... 1 pair of Looms, 3 pair of Shears, 2 pair of Combs and other materialls belonging to the trade £4, Mault and Wheat £1 10s 0d.*

Morton was clearly a weaver-farmer of the type more common further north. Descending through the buttery, the appraisers turned to the 'Bar(r)n at the Waterside', where they noted

> *Sacks with Oats in them £1 16s 0d, Sadles and Horse gears 13s 0d, Measures and 2 Horse Harrows 10s. 0d.*

In the 'Barn at Langsett' they recorded two carts, a wain, three sleds, a plough and four bags for carrying corn, worth in all £3 14s 0d, and after listing the contents of 'the old house near Waterside' they noted

> *Lime upon the ground at Langsett £4 15s 0d, the Lease and Tenant right of the housing and farm at the Waterside with Lime and Manure thereon £30, Corn and Hay £10, 4 Cows 2 Bullocks £16, 1 Horse £2 10s 0d, 102 Sheep £20.*

Morton had £4 in ready money and £314 5s 4d in 'Moneys owing by bonds and otherways'. The total value of his personal estate was £465 9s 0d.

Ordinary farmers were known as husbandmen, but from their inventories it is often difficult to distinguish them from the yeomen. On 15 April 1726 the personal estate of Peter Lindley of Dean Head, husbandman, began with a record of his possessions in his house, two parlours, chambers, stable, barn and wain house. At that time of year

Dean Head barn, a view that Peter Lindley would have been familiar with nearly three hundred years ago.

he had only a little unthrashed corn, hay and straw, but his manure and the seed he had sown were valued at £9 5s 0d and his farm equipment at £7 13s 6d. His livestock comprised

> *1 pigg 2 heiffers with Calf, £6 9s 0d. 2 Stirks a Drape* [barren] *Cow a Cow a Calf, £10 10s 0d. 4 Stears 2 Calves 60 Sheep, £37, 1 Horse £4.*

This compares with the inventory of a yeoman, Emanuel Rich of Catshaw Cross, taken on 14 April 1719:

> *Corn £4 12s 6d, Hay £1 10s 0d, 5 bease and 2 horses, £20 5s 0d, Sheep £6 14s 0d, bees £1 5s 0d, Manure and coals 4s 6d.*

and farm equipment worth £4 10s 0d. When a contemporary husbandman, Joshua Lindley of Hunshelf, died in May 1719, his inventory recorded farm equipment worth £9 7s 10d and

> *A pigg 11s 0d, 49 old Sheep and 18 Lambs £15 5s 0d, 2 Oxen 4 Stears 4 year old Sterks a heffer and Calf 2 Spring calfs 3 Cows 2 horses, £5 10s 0d, Manure £2 10s 0d, 22 acres Corn £37.*

The inventory of the personal estate of Joshua Hinchliffe of Carlecoates, taken on 15 August 1734, does not tell us whether his neighbours thought of him as a husbandman or yeoman, but it gives a full list of his livestock and crops and the equipment that he used on his farm at the edge of the moors:

> *Two Coulters and a Share 4s 0d, Seventy Five Ewes £22 10s 0d, Fifty six Lambs £9 16s 0d., Sixty Wethers £22 10s 0d, Twenty Seven Weathers £7 8s 6d, Three Cows £6 6s 0d, One Cow £1 10s 0d, Three Calves £1 12s 0d, Four Stirks £4 4s 0d, Two Cows £1 11s 0d, Four Oxen £12, Two Heifers £3 5s 0d, Two Horses £6, A Wain £5, Twenty Four Daywork of Corn £26 8s 0d, Seventeen Acre of Hay £10 15s 0d, Two Ropes 3s 0d, Three Sleds and Sides and barrs 6s 6d, Four Harrows 18s 0d, Two Ploughs 10s 0d, A Wain 15s 0d, Two Pack Sadles 4s 0d, A Hackne Sadle 2s 6d... Two Garths and two Wantoes 2s 0d, Three Yokes and Lans 7s 0d, Two Teames 4s 6d, Two Wheel Barrow Sides 6d, A pair of Iron Geers Barr and Haims 3s 0d, A pair of Hemp Gears Barcum and Haims 1s 0d, A Muck Dragg 6d, A Spade 1s 0d, A Hack 1s 0d, Three Stees 2s 0d, Two Plough Beams 2s 0d, Fifteen Geese 12s 6d.*

Many of the terms used are no longer familiar to us. A wether was a castrated ram. A hackney saddle was for riding, the garths and wantoes were straps to secure a pack on a horse and lanes, hames and teams were various straps or harness. A stee was a ladder.

The weavers were not the only craftsmen to combine their trade with running a small farm. When William Barber, the Denby blacksmith, died in December 1697, his appraisers found

1 paire of Bellows 1 steathey [anvil] *vice Hamers and other Iron £2*

in his smithy, ten shillings worth of wool and yarn in a chamber, farm equipment worth £9 15s 0d, a milkhouse, and

26 sheep Wheat and Blendcorne in the Lath [a mixture of wheat and rye in the barn] *£14, 21 days worke of Oats, Peas and Barley in the Lath 2 Oxen 2 Steares £51 10s 0d, 3 Cowes 2 Heffers 1 calfe 1 Horse 2 Mares £22 10s 0d, 2 Swine… 3 Loads 1 mett of seed wheat for a day's ploughing £2 3s 0d, 3 Load of Lime and hustlement £3 10s 0d.*

When John Priest, a later Denby blacksmith, died in December 1717, his appraisers found

Money and gold found in several Boxes £40. Bonds and a bill, £144 10s 0d.

The contents of his smithy were listed as

vice 13s 0d, bellows and things belonging them £1 5s 0d, 2 Stythies £2 5s 0d, 1 litle Stythie 1s 2d, 7 hammers and 1 Axe 5s 0d, 7 pair of tongs 1 poit [poker] 1 Scumit [skimmer] 1 Ladle 5s 0d, all the old Iron and horse 8 hoes 4s 0d, New Iron 5s 0d, Divers Implements for Working 16s 0d, 2 Grinding Stones 2s 6d, 1 hack 1 Spade and Gavelock [crowbar] *5s 0d.*

After valuing his farm equipment at £4 6s 0d, the appraisers noted

6 beasts, viz. 3 Cows 1 Why [heiffer] *and two Calfs £10 10s 0d, 1 horse £3 10s 0d, a old Mare £1. Corn and hay in the Laith £10 10s 0d. 1 Swine 16s 0d. 2 Days plowing of Wheat Sown £1 6s 0d.*

Priest's family also earned extra income from the textile trade; three spinning wheels were recorded and 'Shop goods: Cloth and Spikes etc.' were valued at £39 9s 10d.

Another metalworker, Robert Camm of Roughbirchworth, had 'Wire and all working tools, £1, A Maul Cowlrake, 1s 6d, Coals 14s 0d' recorded in his workshop when an inventory was taken on 2 October 1728. His farm equipment was valued at £3 15s 0d saddles in his barn at, 5s 0d and the rest of his farm stock as follows:

8 acres Oats, £12, Wheat £1, 8 acres hay £6, Manure £2, Lime £1 16s 0d. 1 Bay Gelding £3 10s 0d. I Grey Gelding £2, 1 black swine 14s 0d, a pair of Oxen £9 15s 0d, 1 black Cow 12s 6d, 1 brown Cow

£1 10s 0d, 1 heifer £2 15s 0d, 1 black Calf 12s 6d, 50 sheep £10.

These lists of personal estate were taken by three or four neighbours who had sworn on solemn oath to make 'a true and perfect inventory', which was then attached to the will. Drawn up in an age when spellings were not yet standardised and when local speech included many words that are no longer in use, these documents provide fascinating insights into the living conditions and farming practices of the late-Stuart and early-Georgian era. The full inventory of John Cooke of Oxspring, husbandman, taken on 21 June 1701, serves as an example:

His purse and Apparrell £2.
House: 1 Range 1 fireshovel 1 pair of Tongs, 3 Iron pots 2 brass pots, 1 brass pan, 1 brass Kettle, 2 brass prigs 1 brass Ladle 1 pair of Racks 1 Spitt £3 2s 6d, 1 frying pan 1 dripping pan and a Bill 1 Line Heckle 2 Smoothing Irons 7s 0d, 1 Cupboard 1 Table with Forms 1 Lang Settle, 1 little Table 2 buffitts £2 15s 0d, 4 Chairs 1 little Table 1 dresser 1 dish and Cratch 6s 0d, 10 pewter dishes 1 Candlestick 1 porringer 1 Tumbler 1 Saucer 13s 8d.
Little Parlor: 1 Seeld bed 1 Feather bed, 1 Chaff bed, two blanketts 2 Coverletts, 2 Sheets 1 Fether bolster 2 Fether pillows with drawers Curtains and Valliancs £5, 1 Table 1 Forme 1 Chest 1 Desk 1 Seeld Chaire two buffitts £1 2s 0d, 2 pair of Linnen Sheets 1 pair of Hemp Sheets 3 Course drawers, 1 pair of fine drawers, 2 Table Cloths 7 Table Napkins £1 18s 4d.
Farr Parlor: 2 halfe head beds with bedding £3, 1 Cupboard 1 Chist 1 Chair 1 Arke £1 12s 0d, 1 Side Sadle 2 Ringes 14s 10d.
Chamber: 1 Seeld bed with bedding £1, 1 Halfe headed bed with certaine bedding £1, 1 Chist 1 great Arke £1, 1 Kimlin 12s 0d, 2 Wheels 7 Sacks 1 Window Cloth 4 Riddles 1 Cilne 17s 6d, Certain Boards and other Sawn Wood £2, 2 Arks 1 Kneading Trough 2 peashooks 5 pitch Forks 11s 0d, 4 load of Wheat £1 12s 0d, Wood Vessells, 3 Tables 1 Tunnell, 1 Churne, 3 Barrells, 2 Kits, 1 Flaskitt a Bakebroad a Spittle and a Flackitt 15s 0d, 1 Pillion Seat 1 Stroack a halfe peck 1 Mustard ball 2 Iron Wedges 1 Wain Rope 7s 6d.
Buttery: 1 press certain Milk Vessells 1½ dozen Trenchers 1 Hand baskett 15s 0d.
2 Cart wains 1 Shilved Waine £7 10s 0d, 2 plows 1 pair of Ox Harrows, 1 Ox Sled £1 13s 0d, Certain Husbandry Geere 7s 6d, Six Yoakes 4 Teams 2 pair of Lanes £1 3s 0d, 3 pair of Horse Geers 8s 0d, 1 pack sadle 1 Hair Rope 1 Bridle 4s 10d, 1 Ark 7s 0d, 1 Gavelock 1 Hack 1 pick 1 Ax 1 Hatchett 4s 2d.

1 pair of Oxen £12, 1 pair of Steers £9, 2 Cowes £7 10s 0d, 1 Stirk and 1 Whye Stirk £3, 2 Heffers £4, 3 Calves £3 5s 0d, 1 Horse and a Mare £7 13s 4d, 5 Sheep £1 2s 0d.

Corn Sown: 3 Load of Wheat £1 7s 0d, 9 Sacks of Oats £2 5s 0d, 13 Stroak of Barley 14s 0d, 8 Stroak of Peas 8s 0d, a Fromity Wheat Trough 1s 0d, 2 stone Troughs 2 Swine Troughs and 1 Grindlestone with certaine Huslement 10s 0d.

Total: £96 0s 10d.

Debts out of the estate £6.

John Street, John Mokeson, Daniel Walton, Jonathan Cook.

Many of the terms used in the inventory need explanation. A 'prig' was a small pan of brass or iron and the line heckle was for preparing flax for spinning. A 'lang settle' was a long seat with a high back, while a 'cratch' was a rack for holding bacon from the roof. The 'porringer' was an earthenware vessel for porridge. The 'seeld bed' was panelled. The 'cilne' was perhaps a malt kiln. The 'tunnell' was a funnel, the 'flaskitt' a linen basket, and the 'flackitt' a flask made of wood or leather. The 'stroak' and 'peck' were dry measures, the 'trenchers' wooden plates. 'Fromity' was wheat boiled in milk, with sugar or spice added. 'Huslement' meant the bits and pieces that had been missed and which were given a notional value.

Elihu Dickenson's house, High Flatts. Built in 1717, it stands next to the Quaker meeting house.

Inventories of personal estate survive also for some of the men who lived by the new market place in Penistone. John Greaves was described as a butcher in his will, but as inn keeper by the appraisers of his inventory on 21 August 1719, for he kept the *Rose and Crown*. The inn consisted of the house, the long parlour and the little parlour, kitchen and old kitchen, two cellars and nine chambers, including one for a maidservant. In the yard were a brewhouse and stables. Greaves's farm equipment was valued at £13 8s 6d, his 'Manure in the fold with some Swine troughs' at £5, his four sows and eight pigs at £4, his corn at £27 and his hay at £15. He also had four oxen, five cows, seven young cattle, two horses and a foal, valued together at £50. Essential to running the inn were 'Malt £5 8s 0d. 1 malt mill £1 10s 0d, Coales £5' and the items recorded in his 'lobby' as

> 1 range 3 working tubs £1 10s 0d, 35 hogsheads and barrels £10 9s 0d, 315 gallons of ale and wine £13 2s 6d brandy £13 4s 0d.

Greaves's neighbour, Mr Richard Wordsworth, mercer and grocer, had goods in his shop and warehouse valued at nearly £162 in 1724. Three years later, Mr John Ramsden, the schoolmaster, left a modest estate, including books valued at £2, two cows and 'a Rowler in the Garden'. His rooms were described as the house, back kitchen, parlour, cellar, dining room (with two maps and a picture), three chambers and two garrets, together with beds and other goods in the 'Schoolchamber'. He was owed £3 2s 0d for 'Schoolwages and some small rents due'. Other inventories contain unexpected items, such as the 'pair of Tooth Drawers' and 'a Tobacco box' that John Rich, a Thurlstone yeoman, owned upon his death in 1700.

Farming at the time of parliamentary enclosure

Rennie, Brown and Shirreff's Board of Agriculture report, *General View of the Agriculture of the West Riding of Yorkshire* (1793), contains some interesting observations about farming in Penistone parish on the eve of the enclosure of the extensive commons and wastes. The reporters found that in the Penistone district the climate was 'cold and backward to vegetation', the soil 'very variable, but mostly wet and spongy, and a great deal of moor carrying little but heath'. The farms were small, except upon the moors, and 'Mr Bosville of Gunthwaite, the representative of one of the oldest families in the county', was the only large owner. In the vicinity of the town about half the land was ploughed, but much of the parish consisted of moorland. Ploughing was done by four horses, yoked in a line, for by that time few oxen were used. The cereals that were grown were oats

nby Chap

G. Bosville Esq.

Gunthwaite Hall Brock

Cal

Pashley Green Over H.

Rawtun H.

Lane Head

Em Hurst

Ingburch worth

Gother Bottom

Roger Dye G.

Carr Head

Cat Hill

Fell Lane

New House Thorpe

West

Hoyland Swaync

Tinker House

Rodmer

Folly

High Royd

Rodmer

Thurlstone

Hecly

Willy House

Orspring

Wall Hill

Horn thwaite

Cross Royde

Bower Hill

Head

Hill Side

Syles

DENISTON

Cubley

Rough Burchworth

Hartcliff Clump

Royd Fields

Bilcliff

Bleak Royd

Dison Coite

Alderman's Head

Snowden Hill

Jud Fields

Black Moo

Sheep Ho

Under Bank

Midhope Chap

Hunshelf Bank

Shaw Ho

Brooks Bank

Langley Brook

Green

and a small quantity of wheat, but seed time and harvesting were late and sometimes the harvest was not gathered until November. Dung was chiefly applied to the meadows that were cut for hay and it was common practice to spread two chalders of lime per acre over fallow land. Farmers were generally prevented by their leases from paring and burning their turf, but this method was 'thought a great means of improvement upon some lands'. Much of the land needed draining, but the proper method of doing it was not well understood. The report advocated the enclosure of the common moors, with 'every man's property laid by itself'.

In 1801, fearful of the impact of the war with France, the government ordered a survey of the acreages devoted to each crop.[12] The curate of Penistone wrote:

> *Tho' the parish of Penistone is very extensive yet there is little land upon the Plow in Comparison, the Farms in general being grazing and Stock Farms.*

He estimated that in his parish the crop of oats covered 1,412 acres, wheat 753, turnips 197, barley 118, peas 31, potatoes 23, rye 6 and beans 4.

Rennie, Brown and Shirreff identified the long horned cattle of Penistone parish as being 'of the Derbyshire breed, which are smaller than the Craven breed'. They gave a much fuller description of the characteristic 'Penistone' breed of sheep:

> *The sheep bred upon the moors in the western part of the Riding, and which, we presume, are the native breed, are horned, light in the fore quarter, and well made for exploring a hilly country, where there is little to feed them, but heath and ling; these are generally called the Peniston breed, from the name of the market town, where they are sold. When fat they will weigh 10 lb to 15 lb per quarter. They are a hardy kind of sheep, and good thrivers. When brought down, at proper age, to the pastures in the low parts of the country, they feed as cleverly, and are as rich mutton as need be. We suppose crossing ewes of this sort with a [Robert] Bakewell ram, would produce an excellent breed for the low country pasture, as the Bakewell kind have the properties that the Peniston wants. ... Those bred above Peniston are well adapted to those uncultivated barren mountains.*

'Penistone' sheep are now more generally known as 'Whitefaced Woodlands'. Their characteristic features are a white face and legs, pink nostrils and a muscular tail. Their wool is rather harsh and of medium length and is clipped to about four to five pounds a fleece.

The extensive commons and wastes of Penistone, Langsett and Midhope, shown on Thomas Jeffreys's map of Yorkshire (1772), forty or fifty years before their enclosure.

By 1964 the breed was in danger of extinction and so was included in the gene bank kept by the Zoological Society of London at Whipsnade, but in 1971, after an absence of twenty years, classes were again held for this breed at Penistone Show and they now number about 3,000.[13]

The views expressed in Rennie, Brown and Shirreff's report were echoed in 1822 by Edward Baines's *Directory of the West Riding*. Baines thought:

> *the environs of Penistone have a dreary and barren appearance, especially to the Westward, where nothing presents itself to the eye but black and barren moors, covered chiefly with heath and ling... The climate, as well as the soil, is cold and unfavourable to vegetation.*

Fifteen years later, John Holland commented, in his Tour of the Don:

> *The situation of Peniston is peculiarly bleak and exposed; and the cultivated tract by which the town is surrounded, was formerly remarkable, not more for the paucity of its produce, than for the lateness of the period at which the crops commonly yielded to the influence of the gentler seasons... [especially] about Langsett, where oats might have been standing in stooks upon the field, late in the month of November last year.*

However, he considered that:

> *Of late years, the agricultural aspect of the neighbourhood appears to have undergone a striking change for the better.*[14]

Between 1800 and 1826 the extensive commons and wastes of Penistone parish were enclosed by six private Acts of Parliament. Because the commons were so large and the boundaries were complicated and sometimes disputed, the commissioners and their surveyors often took a long time to sort out all the rival claims. The Act to enclose the commons of Ingbirchworth was passed in 1800 but the award was not made until 1813. The other Acts and awards covered each of the remaining townships: Denby (and Clayton West) 1800-4, Hunshelf 1810-13, Langsett 1811-14, Thurlstone 1812-16, Oxspring 1818-26 and Penistone 1819-26.[15] Immediately after the publication of an award, the owners of the new 'allotments' employed labourers to build those characteristic straight, drystone walls that enclose the fields and lanes of large parts of the parish. Within a generation, the landscape of Penistone parish was transformed by these new fields.

Thomas Jeffreys's map of 1772 shows how little of Penistone parish

An aerial view of Doubting and Mossley Farms showing the fields that were created at the time of the enclosure of the commons and wastes of Langsett township, 1811-14. The 'dumb-bell' shaped fields were an experiment of William Payne, Lord of Langsett, to provide shelter for livestock from all directions.

was cultivated when compared with the huge amount of unfenced common grazing. Thurlstone township contained 8,116 acres, of which 6,522 were commons and wastes. No houses had yet been built up High Bank or at Millhouse Green because these places still formed part of the commons. At the other side of the valley common land went all the way up to Hartcliff. In Penistone township the Green extended from the south end of High Street down Green Road and continued as a narrow strip as far as Castle Green. The 298 acres of Penistone Common stretched from Cubley and the medieval clearing known as Joan Royd as far as Mossley Dike, the boundary within Langsett Common. Four of the new fields that were created upon the enclosure of Langsett Common were given

An Edwardian photograph of Penistone Show, with Cammell Laird's steelworks in the background. The Penistone Agricultural Society held its first show in 1854.

distinctive shapes and high walls to protect sheep and cattle in bad weather. They were the idea of William Payne, the Quaker owner of Frickley Hall and a noted agricultural improver, who had bought the manor of Langsett in 1802. Payne received 2,547 acres at the Langsett enclosure award, including the whole 2,045 acres of Langsett High Moors, 66 of the 123 acres of Boardhill Common, 62 of the 113 acres of Swinden Common, and 44 of the 243 acres of Fullshaw Common. Some new farms were created immediately, but in the far western parts of the parish Langsett Moors and Thurlstone Moors could never be brought into cultivation and so were preserved for grouse shooting.

Chapter Five

Religious Dissent
and Bullhouse Chapel

✠

During the middle and later years of the seventeenth century, the parish of Penistone was a stronghold of Protestant Dissent. The leading families in the parish – the Bosvilles of Gunthwaite, the Burdetts of Denby, the Wordsworths of Water Hall, the Riches of Bullhouse and the Micklethwaites of Ingbirchworth – were puritans before and during the Commonwealth and staunch Nonconformists in later times. The Burdetts, Micklethwaites, Riches and Wordsworths had been established in their respective parts of the parish from at least the fourteenth century. Ties of friendship had often been reinforced by marriage. The Bosvilles were a cut above the rest and they chose their marriage partners from much further afield. At the heralds' visitation of 1584 only the Bosvilles and the Burdetts had their coat-of-arms allowed.[1]

The solidarity of religious opinion amongst these prosperous and long-established families was crucial to the continuing strength of Dissent, here as elsewhere, long after the Restoration. As we shall see, national events did little to change the way in which the parishioners of Penistone conducted their church services during the reigns of Charles II and James II. There is just one piece of tantalising evidence to suggest that similar beliefs may have been held by earlier generations of these leading families. In the reign of Queen Mary, Leonard Wordsworth was found guilty of ridiculing Catholic practices. In 1554 he received penance in Penistone Church:

> *for that he did misuse hyme self in the... pulpite, and also that he did misuse hyme selfe otherwise in castinge water in the church after the priest casting holie water.*[2]

Later Wordsworths, including Mary, the mother of Elkanah Rich, the founder of Bullhouse Chapel, were fervent puritans.

The Origins of the Rich Family
By the time that Bullhouse Chapel was built, the Riches were one of

the oldest families in Thurlstone township. They had first appeared in local records in deeds dated 1372 and 1374 and in the poll tax returns of 1379, when William Rich, a mercer, headed the township list with a contribution of 12d tax. At that time, the family was living at Carlecoates, two miles further west than Bullhouse, right on the edge of the moors. In the fifteenth century a later William Rich bought the Bullhouse estate from the Appleyards, another long-resident family who had been recorded in the returns of 1379 and who remained in the locality until Victorian times.[3] The Riches stayed at Bullhouse for more than three centuries.

The Riches can be traced through seven generations from the William Rich of the 1370s to Aymor Rich, who was living at Bullhouse in 1624 when he was chief constable of the wapentake of Staincross, an ancient district dating back to Viking times that stretched from Penistone parish in the west to Hemsworth in the east. Aymor was a Germanic name that had been introduced into England by the Normans and which had long been favoured by the Burdetts of Denby.[4] The Burdetts were old friends of the Riches and had been witnesses to their deeds back in the 1450s. Aymor Rich was the major landowner in Thurlstone township. In addition to Bullhouse, he owned houses nearby at Catshaw, Millhouse and Smallshaw, two corn mills at Bullhouse and Thurlstone, and two fulling mills at Millhouse and Thurlstone. Younger branches of the family were established at these three houses and at Hornthwaite and Parkin House close by.[5]

Aymor Rich had three sons; William lived at Bullhouse, Daniel went to Smallshaw, and Edward set up home at Millhouse. Meanwhile, Aymor's younger brother, Richard, had moved to the Royd, near Smallshaw, where he was succeeded by his son and grandson. Edward's son, Daniel, inherited Catshaw. Each of these properties lay within a mile of Bullhouse. This part of the parish was clearly the territory of the Riches. The collectors of the hearth tax for Lady Day 1672 recorded seven households of Riches in the township of Thurlstone and another in the neighbouring township of Hunshelf. Mr Sylvanus Rich, Aymor's grandson and heir, and the father of Elkanah, headed the list of Thurlstone names with six hearths in his new hall.[6] Three hundred years after the first William Rich, the family was still the wealthiest in the township and one of the most important in Penistone parish.

Puritanism had taken firm root in the parish of Penistone by 1627, when the second Godfrey Bosville and other inhabitants of the townships of Denby and Gunthwaite built a chapel-of-ease at Denby,

Bullhouse Hall. Erected by Sylvanus and Mary Rich in 1655, and extended (to the right) by their son, Elkanah, in 1688, the hall was the finest residence in the western half of Penistone parish.

some three miles north of the parish church, and installed as their minister a zealous puritan, Mr Charles Broxholme. This Godfrey Bosville afterwards moved to Warwickshire, became MP for Warwick in the Long Parliament and was subsequently a colonel in the parliamentary army.[7] His son, William, who succeeded him at Gunthwaite, served in the same army and so did other prominent parishioners. Aymor Rich's son, William Rich, gentleman, was made a captain under Lord Fairfax, in 1644. Another captain in the same army was William's friend and neighbour, Adam Eyre of Hazlehead Hall, the famous diarist, puritan and parliamentarian, whose family had moved from Crookhill in north Derbyshire and who were connected by marriage with the Micklethwaites.[8]

William Rich must have shared Godfrey Bosville's religious beliefs because in the same year that Denby chapel was built he christened his son, Sylvanus. This was one of those Biblical names that were favoured by certain puritans. Sylvanus appears in St Paul's letters, and Silas in the Book of Acts is probably a shortened version of the name. Neither forms had been used in England before the Reformation, but they became popular in the seventeenth century and continued in use in Dissenting circles during the following two centuries.[9] On 22 April 1652, two years after the death of his father,

Sylvanus married Mary, the daughter of Ralph Wordsworth of Water Hall, gentleman. The datestone over the door of Bullhouse Hall shows that Sylvanus and Mary replaced the old house three years after their marriage. Their new home was built in stone in the usual style of the West Riding gentry houses of that period, with gables, mullioned and transomed windows, decorative drip moulds and finials. It was here that their son, Elkanah, was born in 1658 or 1659. They chose his name from the Old Testament; Elkanah was the name of Samuel's father. The name means 'God hath created' or 'possessed by God'.[10]

Elkanah's maternal ancestors were of comparable status to the Riches. The Wordsworths had lived in the parish of Penistone since the late fourteenth century and had recently rebuilt Water Hall in a similar style to Bullhouse. Mary's father, Ralph Wordsworth (1591-1663), was chief constable of the wapentake of Staincross in 1648. Her mother, Elizabeth Micklethwaite of Swaithe Hall, Worsbrough, was a member of the Ingbirchworth family. The celebrated Nonconformist minister, the Reverend Oliver Heywood of Coley in the parish of Halifax, often visited Swaithe and preached at Elizabeth's funeral. Her eldest son, John Wordsworth, who inherited Swaithe, demonstrated his religious beliefs by christening his son Eliasaph (from The Book of Numbers, I, v, 14). Her younger son, Josias (c.1627-1709), inherited Water Hall, Penistone. By that time, junior branches of the Wordsworths were found in many parts of the parish of Penistone and a little further east at Falthwaite in the parish of Silkstone.[11]

Sylvanus Rich and Mary Wordsworth chose to be married at Sheffield, where the vicar and his three assistants were all dedicated puritans. Perhaps Mary was living there at the time, otherwise it is hard to explain why they did not resort to the parish church at Penistone, where the minister shared their views. The Reverend Henry Swift had been appointed vicar in 1649, upon the ejection of the previous incumbent. Colonel Godfrey Bosville was at that time one of the commissioners for the West Riding who were responsible for putting into force the Act for the punishment of 'scandalous clergymen and others'. One of those removed was Christopher Dickenson of Penistone, 'a man of scandalous life and conversation'. Adam Eyre noted how, on 18 March 1647, he went to Broom Hall, Sheffield, the home of a prominent puritan and parliamentarian, William Jessop, JP in the company of

Capt. Rich, Wm. Rich, Ralph Wordsworth, and divers other

parishioners, where we tendred to Mr. Dickinson the somme of £40 upon condicion to leave us according to agreement; but hee refused. Whereupon wee drew a certificate against him, and subscribed it, and I undertooke to carry it to London, and by Mr. Boswell's assistance to assay his removall without money.

The petition against Dickenson included the charges that he was

a common frequenter of alehouses, and of idle company, and hath beene several tymes drunk since his coming to Penistone; and that before his coming thither, and after his entrance into the ministry, he kept a common tipling house.

Another charge was that having announced a day of solemn thanksgiving in the church, he spent the time at Barnsley, 'in tipling and drinking, amongst base lewd company'. The petition was signed by seventy-seven parishioners 'and divers others'; the first signature was that of William Rich of Bullhouse, Elkanah's grandfather. William Rich, Adam Eyre and Ralph Wordsworth again acted on behalf of the parish when they invited Henry Swift to become their minister in January 1649.[12]

Swift was still vicar when Charles II was restored to the throne. After St Bartholomew's Day 1662 ministers who refused to conform to the Church of England were ejected from their livings. Swift was immediately in trouble and in June 1663 was imprisoned for three

Penistone Church, where Henry Swift remained vicar during the reigns of Charles II and James II, though he refused to conform. The chemist's shop was formerly the Cloth Hall, built in 1763.

months at York Castle under the *Five Mile Act*. He and three others were described by the church authorities as 'factious obstinate non-Conforming ministers'. During his time in gaol several ejected Nonconformist ministers preached at Penistone Church on his behalf. The leading inhabitants of the parish remained attached to their beliefs and did their best to protect the Dissenting preachers. The Reverend Nathan Staniforth, who had been ejected from his living at Hognaston (Derbyshire), was given the posts of master of the grammar school and parish clerk, which he retained until a year before his death in 1702.[13]

The Reverend John Crooke was, however, ejected from his cure at Denby upon his refusal to conform in 1662. The untimely death of William Bosville in April that year may have taken away his protector in his hour of need, but perhaps Crooke was not as determined a character as was Swift; he left the parish to end his days in retirement and the post of curate remained unfilled for three years. His eventual successor, the Reverend Timothy Kent, apparently conformed and remained in office until his death in 1691.[14]

Despite being continually harassed for his Nonconformity, Henry Swift remained vicar of Penistone until he died in 1689. After his third spell of imprisonment, his parishioners persuaded him to take the Oxford Oath (1666), by which he promised 'not at any time to endeavour any alteration of government in Church and State'. This pledge was sufficient to keep him out of trouble for a time, but in 1674 he was presented at the archdeacon's court for not burying the dead according to the order prescribed in the *Book of Common Prayer*; for not wearing the surplice when he read prayers and performed the offices; for not bidding holy days; and for neglecting to perambulate the parish bounds at Rogationtide; for preaching without the gown; and for not instructing and examining the youth in their catechisms.[15] Did any other clergyman in England retain his living throughout the reigns of Charles II and James II despite his refusal to conform in so many ways? The living was a poor one, distant from the centres of ecclesiastical and political authority, and therefore perhaps not a matter of great concern to outsiders, but Swift was able to survive chiefly because of the united support of his leading parishioners, who by 1672 included William Cotton, the ironmaster of Wortley Forge, who had moved to Nether Denby.

The ordinary farmers and part-time clothiers of the parish also supported their vicar. As we have seen, seventy-seven of them, together with 'divers others', signed the petition to remove his predecessor. Adam Eyre lent religious books and pamphlets to members of the Appleyard, Coldwell, Greaves, Haigh and Milnes families who lived in various parts of the township of Thurlstone.[16] They may have been equally as committed in their faith as were their gentry neighbours. We cannot assess the strength of Dissent in the parish from the Compton ecclesiastical census of 1676 because Swift did not fill in the returns, but the Reverend Oliver Heywood spoke to large congregations upon his visits to Penistone.[17] In 1666 Heywood observed that:

> *the publick liberty of ordinances is maintained at Peniston now near 4 year after our black Bartolomew day; the providence is the more remarkable considering that Sir Francis Wortley in the warre time kept that church as a garrison for the king, tho he did him no good, but from thence roved up and down the country robbing, and vexing many honest people, -- and now the good people from all parts flock thither and there are sweetly refreshed with the bread of life in publick, when a spiritual famine is through the land.*

Penistone was one of the first churches in which Heywood preached after his ejection from his living at Coley. His journal records:

> *Sunday 15 May 1664: ... going to Peniston to hear Mr Swift, who to this day enjoyeth his liberty (excepting a three months imprisonment). He importunately urge me to preach, which I was over-intreated to doe... the auditory was much affected... for it was a great assembly, and many came very far.*

> *23 April 1665: ... preacht at Peniston... a very great congregation.*

> *5 Nov. 1665: I preacht at peniston and on the wednesday after kept the monethly fast for the plague in London. Notice was brought into the church that some troopes were waiting at the church-gates to apprehend me, but I was guided a back way to my lodging at Water-hall.*

He continued to preach at two monthly intervals in Penistone Church to large congregations and at private meetings nearby. On 9 August 1677 he

> *lodged at Bulloughs with Mr Rich, the day after being thuesday we kept a solemne fast at Leanard Appleyards who hath been long distempered, where were several ministers and there I preacht.*

On Friday, 31 June 1670 he went

> *to Mr Sotwells of Cat-hill, stayed there studying till lords day morning, thence went to Peniston, preacht all day quietly in the church where*

there was a numerous congregation, -- on munday I dined with Mr. Nailour, at Ecklands, went that night to Mr Riches home at Bulloughs, on thuesday visited Widow Street at Langset, came back to Cawthorne late... Mr Cottons at Moore-end.

On 29 August 1678:

Mr Hancock and I preacht at Mr Richs house at Bulloughs, had a full assembly, some assistance, lodged there.

And on 10 April 1684:

Mr Baxter and I spent a solemne day of fasting and prayer at Mrs Richs at Bullows.

Heywood was the most celebrated Nonconformist preacher in the West Riding; the men who spoke with him at Bullhouse were Nathaniel Baxter and Rowland Hancock, two other ejected ministers. As a young man, Elkanah Rich must have often attended prayer meetings, many of them in his own home. His father, Sylvanus, took advantage of the temporary toleration allowed under the *Act of 1672* to license Bullhouse Hall as a meeting-place, with the Reverend Nathan Denton as preacher. The houses of Thomas Haigh of Hazlehead and William Cotton of Denby were licensed at the same time. Nathan Denton was active in many parts of South Yorkshire after his ejection from the living at Bolton-upon-Dearne. In 1690-92 he was said to be 'att Bolton upon Dern preaching abroad at Sundry places'. His son, Daniel, 'lives with his father and preacheth at Severall places'. Daniel was soon to become the first minister at the chapel that Elkanah Rich built at Bullhouse in 1692.[18]

Life at Bullhouse was not always lived at this elevated level, however. The diary of Adam Eyre shows that historians have sometimes over-emphasised the clash of cultures between the chapel and the alehouse. Eyre regretted his frequent visits to alehouses only when he stayed too long. Oliver Heywood wrote these words of censure in his journal for Saturday, 31 October 1674:

being at Wakefield Fair Mr Sylvanus Rich of Bulloughs in Penistone being in Wakefield with Mr Sotwell and others, and having drunk too liberally, they got on horseback the night being dark, but Mr Rich being mounted on a good mare outrid his company and came close down towards Wakefield Bridge. There was a great flood, waters were lying out, so they rode deep before coming to the bridge and went below it to the river, which some imagine was five, others seven yards deep. He kept on though sometimes nearly fell off. They were both taken a quarter of a mile down the water. At last the mare came to the other side in the fields but could not mount out of the water. He caught hold of a bough, was parted from his beast, the bough failed him, he got hold of another, stuck there and at last got out, and at last espied his mare had got into a field. He went to her, got on and rode towards Pomfret, lights of a house, went to bed, got his clothes dryed so came home the Sabbath day. I pray god it may awaken conscience. This man hath made a profession, entertained ministers and meetings at his house, but of late hath given over. Often stayed out late, comes home in the night ventures through dangerous waters Lord strike home by this Providence.

Sylvanus Rich died in 1683, aged fifty-six, and was buried in the parish church at Penistone. Elkanah was the only one of his five children to survive him. The eldest children, Mary and Martha, had died at the ages of ten and one, and two younger boys, each named Theophilus, had lived to be only four and one. Their mother lived to the age of seventy-two and was buried with her husband in 1704. When Elkanah came into his inheritance at the age of twenty-four, he had already been married three years.

Elkanah Rich and Bullhouse Chapel

The strength of Elkanah Rich's religious beliefs is demonstrated by his choice of marriage partners, both of whom were daughters of ejected ministers. On 20 October 1680 he married Margaret, the youngest daughter of the Reverend John Shaw, one of the most famous puritan preachers in the North. John Shaw had been born at Sykehouse in the chapelry of Bradfield, just a few miles away from

Bullhouse Chapel, erected in 1692 by Elkanah Rich, whose hall can be seen in the background.

Bullhouse. He had been vicar of Rotherham and a noted preacher in London, York and Hull, and had donated a copy of Foxe's *Book of Martyrs* to the parish church at Penistone. Margaret had a marriage portion of £600. Her first two children (who were named after her father and her mother) died young, but Mary (who was named after Elkanah's mother) grew up to marry John Hatfield, gentleman, the head of a prominent puritan family from Laughton-en-le-Morthen in another south Yorkshire wapentake.[19]

Margaret, Elkanah's first wife, died on 10 June 1684. Elkanah married a second time the following year, this time choosing Martha, the daughter of the Reverend Richard Thorpe of Hopton, in the parish of Mirfield about ten miles to the north of Bullhouse. She brought a marriage portion of £800. Their children Sylvanus, Elkanah, Richard and Elizabeth all died young, but a son, Aymor, and a daughter, Martha, grew up to survive their parents. Martha took as her first husband, Richard Rodes, esquire, of Great Houghton, whose grandfather had built a chapel in the grounds of his hall in 1650 and had installed a puritan minister. Her second husband was another Dissenter, Samuel Crompton of Derby, esquire. As we shall see, a daughter of her first marriage eventually inherited the estate at Bullhouse.[20]

Elkanah Rich was thirty years old when the Reverend Henry Swift died on 31 October 1689. The vicar's tombstone in Penistone churchyard reads:

> *Here was interred the body of Mr. Henry Swift, November 2nd, 1689, aged 66 years, and having been minister at Peniston forty years.*

His death brought to an end the Dissenters' control of church services at Penistone.

The crucial question of who held the right to present the next vicar was not easy to answer and gave the Crown the excuse to intervene. The Bosvilles once had the right to the presentation, but it had then become divided between four co-heiresses. In 1689 no one was sure where the right of presentation rested because the descendants of the co-heiresses had all died. The Crown therefore presented; twenty-seven years passed before another vacancy occurred, by which time the head of the Bosville family had been accepted belatedly as the rightful person to present to the living.

Before the Crown stepped in, the parishioners had approached the Reverend Robert Meeke, the minister of Slaithwaite chapel, a few miles further north. Meeke noted in his diary:[21]

[6 Feb. 1689/90] ... *there came a man with two letters to desire me to go and preach at Penistone, (their minister being dead) for they desire I should be their vicar. I promised to preach, but as for residing with I would consider on it. Lord direct me! I have no inclination at present to remove.*

[14 Feb.] *This morning I went towards Bullhouse. At Holmfirth, met a man who came to guide me over the moors. About 4 o'clock came to Bullhouse, a place where I never was before.*

[15 Feb.] *Stayed all day at home discoursing with Mr. Riche and some other company, who were earnest with me to be their minister. I gave some reasons against their request, but they seemed unsatisfied and still urged me.*

[16 Feb.] *Preacht at Penistone from John iii, 5. At night some desired me to baptize a child which I did. At noon, dined at Waterhall, returned back to Bullhouse.*

[25 Feb.] *Sent a letter to Mr. Riche, in answer to their request about my going to Penistone; I gave a negative, being at present well settled.*

The Crown chose the Reverend Edmund Hough as the new vicar. It was no doubt with some apprehension that Josiah Wordsworth and Elkanah Rich, 'patrons of Penistone church', presented Hough to the archbishop of York on 21 March 1690. Hough entered his living two months later. Joseph Hunter described him as

a man of considerable learning and attainments, [who] *is said to have kept the town and parish in great awe and order.*

He remained vicar until his death in 1717.[22]

The *Toleration Act* of 1689 brought timely relief to those parishioners who did not welcome the new order. The justices of the peace meeting at the West Riding Quarter Sessions held at Leeds on 19 July 1689 accepted that

a congregation of Protestant Dissenters doe assemble to worship God publickly at the house of Mr. Elkanah Rich, called Bullhouse in Penistone.

The signatures on the petition were those of Francis Haigh and Isaac Wordsworth.[23]

Elkanah wrote to his cousin, Aymor Rich of Smallshaw, regarding his pew in Penistone Church:

my father, mother and myself always sat there in Mr. Swift's time, that

Bullhouse Chapel with the former minister's cottage to the rear.

is while we went to the Church, until they carried things so high and were so full of ceremonies that we resolve to provide a better way of worship at home. I shall therefore not sit there as they manage the Church, but if you like their doings, I had rather you sat there than any other person.[24]

Determined as he was to go his own way, Elkanah apparently respected the views of those who wished to worship according to the rites of the Established Church, even if they were members of his own family.

At the Quarter Sessions meeting in April 1692 at Pontefract, 'a new house at Bullhouse in Penistone' was registered for Nonconformist meetings. Elkanah Rich had decided to build a chapel in the grounds of his own hall and to appoint a Nonconformist minister to serve there.

The chapel remains in use and its vernacular appearance is unchanged externally, though it has been blackened with the smoke of passing trains on the former Sheffield-Woodhead-Manchester line. It is built as a plain rectangle, with no adornments except for four ball finials, which are similar in style to one on Elkanah's extension to Bullhouse Hall. The walls are of large blocks of local millstone grit, the roof is low-pitched and covered with heavy stone slates. Round-headed windows divided by mullions and transomes provide a suitable 'ecclesiastical' touch. The entry is through a stone porch and a wooden door which is heavily studded with large, square-headed nails. Above, is a datestone which reads: 18 April 1692. Inside, three great wooden beams on stone corbels support the ceiling, and the walls have plain, unvarnished oak panelling, some of it made from former box-pews. At one time, the walls were colour-washed, and the wooden floor which replaced the old flags rose in steps towards the back windows. The chief feature of the chapel has always been the pulpit, for the Preaching of the Word was considered the most important part of the service. It is set high and its sounding canopy gives it dignity.

The vestry at the north-western end of the chapel is the original minister's cottage, a simple one-up, one-down building with a tall chimney and a trap door that can be wound up to seal off the upper compartment. The first minister, the Reverend Daniel Denton, MA, was here until his death on 18 February 1721. He was buried in the chapel yard. These early years formed the greatest era in the history of Bullhouse Chapel. In John Evans's *List of Dissenting Congregations* in 1715 the congregation at Bullhouse was said to number 200. Some of these worshippers no doubt came from a considerable distance, nevertheless the figure is an impressive one which attests to the continuing strength of Independency in the parish of Penistone.[25]

Meanwhile, Elkanah Rich had enlarged Bullhouse Hall by adding a wing with a large gable to the right of the entrance. His initials and the date 1688 are carved on a door lintel which has been re-used in

Bullhouse Hall, showing Elkanah Rich's extension to his parents' house. He was responsible for many of the surviving buildings at Bullhouse.

the long, nineteenth-century range which projects forward on the other side of the house. He also built a banquet house in 1686 and the nearby Bullhouse Lodge in 1687, which has been restored in recent years to its former glory. These were years of heavy expenditure, which were later to take their toll, but they helped to assert Elkanah's social position. He was described as 'gentleman' when he served on the grand jury at the West Riding Quarter Sessions held at Sheffield in 1700.[26]

Upon the death of Daniel Denton, Elkanah was despondent about the future of his chapel. He wrote to another member, John Haigh:[27]

My dear and Christian Friend,
I hope you have all of you many serious thoughts of the great and awful breach it has pleased the Lord to make upon us by the death of the worthy and never to be forgotten Mr. Denton. God knows and our conscience will tell us if we make a faithful inquiry how we have prized and improved his excellent Ministry. We have all of us been faulty in this matter and some of us (I fear) very much so. It is now therefore our duty to be very deeply humbled for what has been amiss in the midst of us, and speedily to reform as we expect the Gospel in its power and purity to be continued unto us. What I have done in building the chapel and for the maintenance of the Ministry in this place I need not tell you nor need I mention how little has been done by others, because nothing has been done at all except by two or three persons. When Mr. Denton came here at first I was both able and willing to allow him his table, a horse keeping, and £20 a year in money. But since when I had many children to maintain, considerable sums to pay upon the marriage of my daughters and had been at near £2,000 charge in building. I was obliged to borrow a great deal of money and so was not able to make good the £20 a year to Mr. Denton, which he was so sensible of that he was willing to make a considerable abatement. Now, after all that I have done I will for the future allow £10 per year to a minister in money, his table and horse keeping or one of my own when he has occasion to go abroad. I hope you will think this a good allowance from me, but not a sufficient encouragement to a Minister of worth, bearing an parts to fix with us, such an one we have had, and such an one we will have, or I will in my old age leave the place, but I hope better things. You know that in all other places, Dissenting Ministers are supported by the free gifts of their people, and that it has not been so in this place is what you cannot find elsewhere. Now not to trouble you or myself with words more than are now necessary, the matter in short is this: Appoint two such persons as you think proper

and fit to go about amongst us and see what everyone will freely subscribe to give a Minister and let them begin with me, and when that is done we shall know what prospect we have of supporting religion and the work of the gospel in this place. What I have now written I shall I hope follow with my serious and fervent prayers to the God of all grace and mercy that he would be pleased effectually incline our hearts to do and follow those things which make for the present, future and eternal peace and salvation of our own souls and the souls of ours, and to this end that we may obtain and maintain an able and faithful Minister to Fix and reside with us.

I am, dear Friends
Your affectionate friend and servant
Elk. Rich.

Dear Friend,
I wrote this in March and laid it aside until now which I begin to think was too long a delay. You are the fittest person to see what our people will freely do in this great affair. I beg, therefore, you will undertake it and take one with you which you judge most proper. James Rigby and Caleb Roebuck soon after Mr. Denton's death did offer to do it, but put them off doubting somewhat of their fitness. John Hadfield lately I am told, intimated hiss willingness to go with you on this occasion but I leave that to your discretion.

I am, your affectionate cousin,
Elk. Rich,
Bullhouse, June 16th 1721.

Elkanah died three years later, at the age of sixty-five, and was buried inside his chapel, alongside his young children.

Elkanah and Martha's son, Aymor Rich (1702-69), inherited the estate at Bullhouse and in time achieved the rank of esquire. In 1722 he had married Grace, the daughter and heir of William Bagshaw of Hucklow, a Derbyshire gentleman from a prominent Dissenting family. She died on 29 December 1724 and their only child, named Elkanah after his grandfather, lived less than two years. Bullhouse Hall must have been a gloomy place at that time, with three deaths in a year. Aymor never re-married and died without issue on 18 November 1769. He was buried in Bullhouse Chapel, next to his wife, his son and his father. His monument describes him as

in his behaviour the accomplished gentleman, in his worldly affairs the man of prudence, and in charity to the poor an exemplary christian.

With his death, eleven generations of Riches, stretching over four centuries, came to an end in the male line. He left Bullhouse to his sister, Martha, the widow of Richard Rodes of Great Houghton. Future owners rarely resided on the Bullhouse estate.

The deaths of Daniel Denton and Elkanah Rich signalled the end of an era. Bullhouse Chapel attracted smaller and smaller congregations (60 in 1743, 40 in 1764) and its ministers are mere names to us.[28] A memorial inside the parish church at Penistone, which reads, 'In memory of the Reverend Mr. Benjamin Shaw, minister of Bullhouse chapel, who died the 28th day of September 1771, aged 48 years', suggests cordial relations between the two places of worship: Shaw had been minister at Bullhouse all his adult life. Numbers increased during the nineteenth century and a successful Sunday School was established, but the members never joined the Congregational Union, nor did they become part of the United Reformed Church. Bullhouse Chapel remains Independent and has celebrated its 300th anniversary.

The decline of Independency in the parish of Penistone is less easy to trace than its rise. Daniel Rich of Smallshaw, John Wordsworth and the Burdetts and Cottons of Denby became Quakers.[29] Others turned back to the Church of England. Godfrey Bosville (1654-1714) and his wife are commemorated by marble monuments in the chancel of Penistone Church. Later members of the Bosville family left Gunthwaite and moved to Thorpe in the East Riding. The Cottons moved to the Haigh in the parish of Darton and the Wordsworths moved to Wadworth, Sheffield and London. Junior branches of the Burdetts, Micklethwaites and Wordsworths continued to live in the parish but they did not have the influence of their seventeenth-century predecessors.

The houses of the old Dissenting families survive in surprising numbers. The Wordsworths' properties at Water Hall and Swaithe, the Micklethwaites' house at Ingbirchworth, and John Sotwell's hall at Cat Hill, together with the sturdy, eleven-bay timber-framed barn built by the first Godfrey Bosville at Gunthwaite and the stables and other outbuildings erected by the third of that name, remain intact. The finest group of seventeenth century buildings, however, comprise the hall, lodge, banquet house and chapel at Bullhouse. A railway cutting and a busy road 200 yards down the lane diminish the former sense of remoteness, but if he were able to return Elkanah Rich would not find the place very different three centuries or so after his intense and busy life there.

The Whitsuntide Gathering at Millhouse in 1914, showing the banners of the Sunday Schools of the West End Primitive Methodists and the Thurlstone Wesleyans.

The Chapel in the 1940s

I started to attend the Sunday School at Bullhouse Chapel at the age of two and went every Sunday that I was able to until we left Catshaw when I was nearly eleven. The chapel there has always been Independent in doctrine and organisation. That doctrine has changed slowly over the years but the members of the chapel have remained resolutely in charge of their own affairs. Unlike other Independent chapels, they never joined the Congregational Union nor the United Reformed Church. They have always been dependent on their own resources. A full-time pastor could no longer be maintained, but a lay-preacher from outside our district, a kindly, lame man named Mr Pearson, more-or-less filled this role. His homely sermons stressed the Christian virtues and were based on bible stories and parables such as that of *The Good Samaritan*. The chapel was not just a place of worship but a social centre, at a time when we had no clubs or youth organisations. The Harvest Festival, the Sunday School Anniversary, the Whitsuntide parades and occasional parties, concerts and outings were the major events of our year.

The pulpit was raised in the centre of the end wall of the chapel, so that the pastor dominated all he surveyed. The congregation faced him from their wooden pews and the choir occupied three rows of tiered seats on either side of the pulpit. Hymn singing was led from an harmonium or from a piano. The walls were bare, but large framed certificates and a photograph of Joseph Bardsley, the long-serving pastor, caught the eye. Hat pegs the size of tent pegs were fixed into a rail around the walls. We could readily grasp the meaning of the old expression for staring eyes: 'Eyes like chapel hat pegs'.

The Sunday School's avowed purpose was to teach the Scriptures. We not only received prizes for good attendance but for our performances in the annual Sheffield Sunday School Union examinations. If we did very well we received William Smith awards and extra merit prizes and certificates, which were presented at Victoria Hall, Sheffield. The Whitsuntide processions of all the local Sunday Schools were the greatest communal event of the year. They were the time for wearing new clothes, ordered from Littlewood's catalogue and measured by their representative. He was the only tradesman who ever entered our house at Catshaw. The joint parades had started way back in 1867. Old photographs show that large crowds always gathered for these events. The banner was unfurled from its long box and raised against the chapel wall. Hefty young men had the privilege of placing it in their shoulder straps and leading the march, whilst others held the ropes that took the strain if a wind blew. We all gathered behind, young ones to the front, and set off for Millhouse and Thurlstone, where we were joined by the West End Primitive Methodists, the Thurlstone Wesleyans, the Particular Baptists and Thurlstone Church. The banners were set against the wall, side by side, while Thurlstone Band led the way with hymn-singing and the various pastors took turns to lead prayers and preach a sermon. A solitary policeman allowed what little traffic there was to pass through the crowd. People met old friends, some of whom had returned for the occasion, and presented their children in their best clothes. Each chapel tried to muster the largest crowd and we laughed at the smaller banners alongside our mighty one. We were silently miffed that our banner had the date 1825, which was when the Sunday School was founded, and not 1692, the foundation date of the chapel, for we knew that only Penistone Church could claim to be older than us. When we were very young, we turned back at Thurlstone, but we were soon old enough to demand the right to march on to Penistone, led by the band. In the High Street we found a much larger crowd and the banners of Penistone Church, Netherfield Congregational Chapel, Spring Vale Methodists and St

A joint Sunday School outing on Broadbent's buses from Millhouse in 1953, including some of the author's friends and relatives.

Paul's Wesleyans. After further hymn-singing, prayers, addresses, and conversations with friends, we caught the bus back, arriving in time for tea and games. The Whit walks continued in the 1950s but then gradually petered out, especially when a new Bank Holiday replaced the traditional one at Whitsuntide. A Pentecost Praise Service in Penistone Church is now held instead.

At Christmas time we went on Sunday School trips to pantomimes at Barnsley, Sheffield and even the Bradford *Alhambra*. We saw Albert Modley, the star of 'Over the Garden Wall', and Reginald Dixon, who was always 'proper poorly'. Our other big event was the annual Sunday School outing to the seaside. Blackpool was the popular choice, but we also went to Southport and Bridlington and on one occasion through the Mersey Tunnel to New Brighton. Broadbent's car hire, taxi, coal merchant and haulage contracting firm at Millhouse Post Office arranged the coaches. On one memorable occasion five coaches were needed to fit us all in. Perhaps that was a joint Sunday School venture involving most of the inhabitants of Millhouse and Thurlstone? Millhouse Institute, which had been built in 1925, was closed in the post-war years, so it is unlikely that the trip was organised from there. The only social events that were not organised by the chapels and churches in the 1940s were the school concerts.

Chapter Six

Penistone Market, Cloth Hall and Grammar School

✠

On Thursdays Penistone takes on a different character from that which it assumes during the rest of the week. Thursday is market day and the central streets are busy. A decision taken three hundred years ago has had lasting effects. But Thursday was not the first choice when Penistone market was founded in 1699. Four hundred years previously a local market had been held on a Tuesday, so this was the day that was favoured for the revival. It soon became clear, however, that Penistone market would never get off the ground unless that day was changed. A market would undoubtedly benefit the people of Penistone, but others feared that it might well harm the market that was held each Wednesday only seven miles away at Barnsley. The Penistoners had to change their day if they were to have any chance of getting their market started.

Penistone Market
In 1698 Godfrey Bosville planned to revive the ancient rights of the manor of Penisale to hold a Tuesday market and an annual 10-12 June fair. His idea was to transfer these rights to a new site by the parish church two miles away at Penistone. His plan immediately ran into firm opposition from the owners of market rights at Barnsley and Huddersfield. Barnsley lay just seven miles away and Huddersfield twelve, so the threat of competition naturally caused them concern. On 10 June 1698, the proposed first day of the fair, an order was signed forbidding the holding of markets and fairs at Penistone.[1] Godfrey Bosville's scheme appeared to have floundered, but he and his fellow parishioners were determined in their resolve. They attempted to placate the people of Barnsley, whose market was held on a Wednesday, by moving the suggested date of the Penistone market from Tuesday to Thursday. Then, petitions drawn up by Nathan Staniforth, the parish clerk and master of Penistone Grammar School, were taken to the surrounding towns, villages, hamlets and isolated farmsteads for signatures that would demonstrate widespread support for a market at Penistone. These

Penistone Market Day, 1906. One of several Biltcliffe photographs of these all-male occasions, it captures some striking poses in the space between the church and the Cloth Hall.

petitions are preserved in the antiquarian collections of John Wilson of Broomhead Hall at the Brotherton Library, the University of Leeds, and are instantly recognisable as being in the distinctive hand of Nathan Staniforth.[2]

A typical petition reads:

We whose names are hereunto subscribed being the principal Gentlemen and Inhabitants of the several Parishes and Towns of Silkston, Thurgoland, Dodworth, Stainbrough, and Hoylandswain, being near adjacent to the Parish of Peniston in the County of York, Do humbly certifie to whom it may concern, That to have a Market at the Town of Peniston aforesaid on Thursday in every week, and a Fair on the Tenth Eleventh and Twelfth of June yearly, will be very commodious to the whole Countrie thereabouts: That the same will be of very great advantage to several parts of the Counties of Chester, Lancaster, and Derby lying next to Peniston afforesaid: And that no

Markets or Fairs near that place are held on the same days. And we further humbly certifie, that we verily believe, that the holding of a Market and Fair at Peniston as afforesaid will be of general advantage to the whole Country, and not prejudicial. In Testimony whereof we have hereunto set our hands this Twenty fourth day of August Anno Domini 1699.

The petition was signed by 150 inhabitants of these townships. Across the Pennines, 171 inhabitants of Manchester and Salford, including the various officers, added their support. Their petition reads:

We whose hands are underput Gentlemen and Inhabitants of the townes of Manchester and Salford in the County of Lancaster Doe hereby certifie whom it may concerne That these townes are very populous and usually are weekly supplyed with wheat and other harde corne out of the West Rideing of the County of York and that Wee Doe believe that if a Weekly Market could be Obtained in the town of Penniston in the said Rideing on the thursday (being a day on which the Market days in the townes next adjoyneing thereunto is not) the same wold be of great service to the townes of Manchester and Salford and parts adjacent and wold save great charges in carrying corne from townes more remote from the said townes of Manchester and Salford And therefore doe humbly desire that a Market Might be granted in the said town of Penniston, Weekly on the said day Witness our hands the fourth day of September Anno dni 1699.

The other petitions were signed as follows:
Stockport and Mottram (125)
[Rural parts of Cheshire] (19)
Glossop, Glossop Dale, Hope Woodlands and Edale (99)
Darton, Kexbrough, High Hoyland, Clayton West, Skelmanthorpe and Cawthorne (105)
Kirkburton, Shepley, Cumberworth, Shelley, Kirkheaton and Emley (224)
Holmfirth and Saddleworth (240)
Wakefield (35)
Sandal Magna (21)
Doncaster (28)
Bolton-upon-Dearne, Barnburgh, Adwick-upon-Dearne and Goldthorpe (30)
Tankersley, Wortley and Pilley (107)
Wentworth, Hoyland, Thorpe Hesley, Scholes, Greasborough, Morley, Haugh, Barrow and Cortworth (72)

The parish of Ecclesfield and the chapelry of Bradfield (308)
Sheffield (72)
Attercliffe, Darnall, Brightside and Tinsley (104)
Penistone parish (230).

In all, 2,140 persons from a wide area around Penistone signed the various documents. For the benefit of the government officials in London, to whom the petitions were presented, the exaggerated claim was made that

> *such was the state of the country between Penistone and Barnsley, their nearest market, that persons had lost their lives in winter time returning home.*[3]

Perhaps this claim was believed, for the application was successful. From 1699 Penistone was able to hold a three-day fair on 10-12 June (the same days as the old medieval fair of St Barnabas at Penisale) and a market every Thursday.

A Market Place was laid out in front of the tower of the medieval church of St John the Baptist. Was there, one wonders, a village green on this site before 1699, or were some properties cleared away? Our

William Fairbank's plan of Penistone, 1749. This simple plan, by the first of four generations of a famous Sheffield firm of surveyors, shows the Market Place that was laid out in front of the church in 1699, before the Cloth Hall was built in 1763.

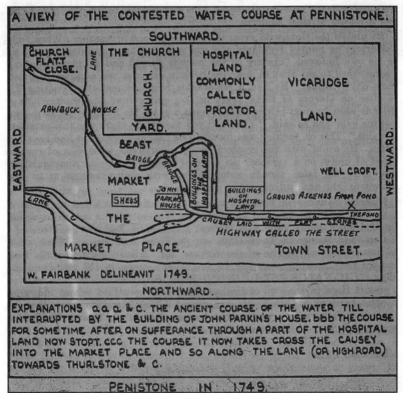

Penistone High Street. Penistone became a shopping centre upon the success of its market. These buildings date from the middle of the nineteenth century.

first evidence of the shape of the new market place comes fifty years after its foundation. A plan drawn up in 1749 by William Fairbank, the Sheffield surveyor, to help resolve a dispute over a water course, shows the 'Beast Market', including 'sheds' and 'John Parkin's house', immediately west of the churchyard.[4] A large stone with the letter 'P' still marks the former north-western corner of Parkin's property. On Fairbank's plan, 'The Market Place' lay west of this building, in the present Market Street. Shrewsbury Road did not exist, so the only way to the east was down Church Hill, to the north of the churchyard.

The effect of the market on Penistone was momentous. The various records that survive from the late seventeenth century show that Penistone had been only a small place. As we have seen, the hearth tax returns of 1672 record only twenty-six householders in Penistone township (though the poor who were exempt from the tax were not listed).[5] The War Office enquiries of 1686[6] had noted that Penistone had only five guest beds and three stables available for visitors, and a local assessment of 1697[7] named only thirty-three householders, with no innkeepers and few tradesmen (though with three clothiers). This situation changed when Penistone was turned into a small market town. It is no coincidence that in 1702, three years after the foundation of the market, the old Penistone Grammar School on the north side of the churchyard was placed on a more ambitious footing with the appointment of John Ramsden, of Batley, as master. The new school building, which included accommodation for boarders, was completed by 1716.[8] Inns and shops soon began to appear around the Market Place. The *Spread Eagle, Old Crown, Rose and Crown*, and *Fleece* (closed 1873), and *Horns Coffee House and Tavern* became busy places on market day. By 1770 the sixth edition of William Owen's *Book of Fairs* was advertising four annual fairs for horned cattle and horses at Penistone, all of which were held on market day (the last Thursday in February, the last in March, the Thursday before old May-day, and the one after old May-day). In 1822 Edward Baines's *West Riding Directory* described Penistone as

> *a small market town. Thursday is the market day, and a good number of cows, calves and sheep are on that day generally exhibited for sale.*

The market and fair that had been established in 1290 at Penisale had failed, but the hopes of Godfrey Bosville and his fellow parishioners in the 1690s had been fulfilled.

The Cloth Hall

Today, the prime site in the former Market Place is occupied by a building which is fronted by Clark's chemist's shop. The building was not there on William Fairbank's plan of 1749, but soon it had a key role in the development of Penistone as a commercial centre. It was erected as a Cloth Hall in 1763, a couple of generations after the foundation of the market, when confidence in the local economy was still high.

Penistone parish lay on the fringe of the West Riding textile district. It had given its name to a distinctive coarse cloth that tailors turned into cheap, serviceable clothes. 'Penistones' were 12-13 yards long, 1¼ yards broad, and weighed twenty-eight pounds. They were similar to other undyed cloths, such as 'Northern

Dozens', which were the same length, but half a yard broader, and thirty-three pounds in weight, and to the more widely-known kerseys, which were only a yard wide, seventeen to eighteen yards long, and which weighed just twenty pounds.[9] When Daniel Defoe visited Stourbridge Fair, on the outskirts of Cambridge, in the early eighteenth century, he observed:

> *Here are clothiers from Halifax, Leeds, Wakefield and Huthersfield in Yorkshire, and from Rochdale, Bury, etc, in Lancashire, with vast quantities of Yorkshire cloths, kerseyes, pennistons, cottons, etc.*[10]

The merchants of the West Riding textile towns included Penistones among their stock. For example, Mr Francis Kellam, a Pontefract mercer and draper who died in 1688, owned '9 yards of Penestone', worth 12s 0d.[11] Further back in time, 'Penistones' were recorded in 1468-69, 'Ordinary Penistones' or 'Forest Whites' and 'Sorting Penistones' were mentioned in Acts of Parliament in 1553, 1554, 1597 and 1607, and a survey of the West Riding textile industry in 1595 noted that 'at Penistone near Barnsley and some villages thereabouts are made about one thousand pieces of White Peny Stones'. These were counted only as half cloths for assize purposes, thus some 500 pieces were made annually.[12] Further information about the extent of the trade in the sixteenth century is provided by records of the searchers at the cloth market held at Blackwell Hall, London, in 1561-62. Lists of fines for defective pieces included the names of 'George Sabell [i.e. Savile], Yorkshire, northern peniston', 'John Blackborne, Yorkshire, peniston' [whom later references show was from Wakefield], and other unnamed Wakefield men who were selling 'penistons', 'peniston dozens' or 'northern penistons'.[13] Finally, a chance piece of evidence from the Elizabethan period comes in a letter written in London in 1587 from Anne Boughton to her father, in which she refers to an acquaintance who would not let his son wear 'a coate of penniston' because it was too hot.[14]

It is clear then that, from at least the fifteenth century, the inhabitants of the parish of Penistone had obtained part of their living through the manufacture of cheap woollen cloth. Inventories of personal possessions that were made when a will was proved depict typical West Riding weaver-farmers, especially in the northern parts of the parish.[15] In 1719 James Beaumont of Denby had a 'wool chamber' and a 'weaving chamber' containing three pair of looms and two pair of combs. In 1725 Matthew Burdett of Nether Denby had a pair of looms, a pair of combs and a warping wough 'with all other things belonging the trade' in his workshop. A piece of kersey cloth and a piece of plain cloth were ready for the cloth hall and his farm stock included cattle, sheep, corn and hay. A more detailed list of the personal estate of William Rowley of Ingbirchworth, clothier, was prepared upon his death in 1763. His packs of wool were valued at £35 19s 8d, two pieces that were dressed and finished were expected to fetch £7 10s 0d, and eight pieces at various stages of production were worth £23 8s 0d. His weaving equipment included a pair of looms and accessories, three pair of shears, four wheels, and 'warping woof, creels and a stool'.

During the eighteenth century, as the West Riding textile industry grew mightily, the inhabitants of several towns decided to build cloth halls, where pieces of cloth could be brought for sale to the merchants. Halifax (1708), Wakefield (1710) and Leeds (1711) led the way. The finest surviving structure is the Piece Hall that was built

Penistone Church, Cloth Hall and Grammar School, the three important buildings at the centre of Penistone. The Cloth Hall had become the printing office of J H Wood, author of Remarkable Occurrences *and the* Penistone Almanacks. *The old Grammar School just appears to the left.*

at Halifax in 1779, with 315 rooms arranged around a central courtyard. The hall is the major surviving monument from the 'domestic economy' stage of the West Riding textile industry on the eve of the Industrial Revolution.

The growth of trade encouraged the parishioners of Penistone to establish their own cloth market. At first, this was held on market days in the upper part of the Grammar School, close to the Market Place. William Spencer of Cannon Hall, Cawthorne, noted in his pocket book: 'attended first day of Penistone Cloth fair, 30 September 1743'.[16] The previous day an agreement had been drawn up under the direction of Aymor Rich of Bullhouse Hall and George Walker of Hunshelf Hall, two of the leading gentlemen of the parish.[17] This was signed at Penistone on 10 November by ninety-two cloth makers. It reads:

Whereas All or the Greatest part of the Clothmakers in and about the parish of Penistone have sometime lately brought their Cloth to Penistone to Sell and having had good Encouragement therein by the Mercers for the Sale of their Cloth And the Greatest part of the Trades people (the Clothiers in that Neighbourhood deal with) being desireous that there may be a Meeting at Penistone Established, And we whose hands and Seals are hereunto sett having Agreed to bring our Cloth to Penistone instead of carrying the same to Sheffield for the better encouragement thereof do Severally and for our Severall own Act and Acts only and not one for the other or for the Act or Acts of the other Covenant promise Grant and Agree to and with Aymor Rich of Bullhouse in the Parish of Penistone in the County of York Gentleman and George Walker of Hunshelf in the Parish aforesaid Gentlemen and either of themy or either of their Executors and Administrators That such of us as shall directly or Indirectly Sell or expose to Sale by ourselves Servants or Agents any Kersey Cloth or Plaines at any Markett or Markett to be held at Sheffield by Swatch 18 or otherways at any time or times on or before the Twenty Ninth day of September next, that such person or persons as shall so Sell or Expose to Sale by themselves or any Person or Persons for them or on their behalf shall well and truly upon demand pay unto the said Aymor Rich and George Walker or the one of them their or the one of their Executors or Administrators the Sum of Three Pounds for every peice of Cloth that such Person or persons shall by themselves or otherways sell or expose to sale at Sheffield aforesaid or at any Markett or Marketts to be held there at any time or times on or before the said Twenty ninth day of September, Witness our Hands and Seals the Tenth day of November in the Year of our Lord One Thousand Seven Hundred and Forty three.

A second agreement was made at the same time by the three local fullers whose mills scoured and felted cloths that had just been woven: John Wood of Oxspring, and Francis Batty and Thomas Hobson of Thurlstone township.[19] They agreed not to treat cloth for any manufacturer who had not entered into the first agreement, thereby effectively preventing anyone from withdrawing their support from the scheme.

The success of the cloth market encouraged the parishioners of Penistone to build a hall that was more commodious than the upper room in the Grammar School. John Platt's *Journal* for March 1763[20] refers to his making a 'Plan for a market house or Cloth Hall at Penistone', and to his discussions with Mr John Hatfield (Aymor Rich's brother-in-law, from Laughton-en-le-Morthen) and Mr Josias Wordsworth of Water Hall and Wadworth Hall, near Doncaster. Platt's design was accepted. Penistone Cloth Hall was built that year at the cost of £800, with Josias Wordsworth heading the subscription list.[21]

John Platt was the son of George Platt, who had moved from Disley (Cheshire) to work in South Yorkshire as an architect and master mason. George Platt was responsible for the gentry halls at Cusworth and Hickleton and supervised the building of St Paul's Church, Sheffield. After George's death, at the early age of forty-three, his son became the leading architect and builder in south Yorkshire. John Platt is known to have designed and built the shambles and butchers' cross at Doncaster (1756) and the Barnsley shambles and market hall (1767). He also worked at Wortley Hall and Wentworth Castle, and was responsible for Thundercliffe Grange, the Feoffees' School at Rotherham, and the rebuilding of Eckington Church.[22] He was the obvious person to turn to for the new Market House and Cloth Hall at Penistone.

It is likely that the large windows of Clark's shop were originally open arches into the Market House and Cloth Hall. We do not know how long the building was used for that purpose. When the Wordsworth estate was sold in 1825 'The Market House' consisted of a dwelling house, a carpenter's shop, two chambers, and several butchers' stalls. By that time, the building may no longer have been used as a Cloth Hall. Penistone lay on the southern edge of the textile district, and the improved communications of recent years had favoured the use of the major Piece Halls further north. Penistone Cloth Hall was gradually converted to other purposes. A room was used by the Barnsley magistrates for meetings of the petty sessions until the 1840s, and during the second half of the nineteenth century the present chemist's shop served as J H Wood's

Penistone Market Place, 1906. A Biltcliffe photograph taken from the upper storey of the Midland Bank, showing cattle in the street and sheep in pens. Two women have dared to intrude upon the scene.

'Post Office and Printing Office'. In 1861 the eastern part of the Cloth Hall was made into a pub called *The White Bear*; when it closed in the 1920s, it became the local home of the British Legion.[23]

The New Market
Meanwhile, the cattle market continued to be held in the streets around the Cloth Hall. Old photographs taken by Joshua Biltcliffe

show that in the early years of the twentieth century market day was a masculine event. Dairy shorthorns were offered for sale in the old Market Place, up High Street and down St Mary's Street, and sheep pens were placed in front of the *Spread Eagle*.

The old custom of adolescent boys and girls offering themselves for annual hire as servants continued in the Market Place until the early years of the twentieth century. These occasions were known as Statute or 'Stattis' hirings (because they were authorised by statute, or *Act of Parliament*) and were normally held in the autumn at Martinmas. At Penistone, the hiring day was the Tuesday before New Martinmas Day. An item headed 'Penistone Statute Hirings' in the *Yorkshire Post*, Wednesday, 8 November 1905 reads:

There was a larger attendance at these statute hirings yesterday than for some years but not many engagements were entered into.

The same paper reported on Wednesday, 9 November 1910 a thin attendance, with very much higher wages sought by all, and on Thursday, 7 November 1918:

at Penistone statute hirings on Tuesday, not one male or female servant offered for hire. [24]

The old system had collapsed during the First World War.

By the early 1900s the Thursday market was causing concern over public health. In June 1903 the Ministry of Agriculture and Fisheries ordered that a new site should be found. The members of Penistone Urban District Council responded in a dilatory fashion as various options were discussed, but finally, on 24 November

The men of Penistone put on their flat caps and rejoice at the opening of the new market in 1910.

1910, a new market under covered shedding was opened in Backfields, at the end of a side-street leading from the Market Place, and the adjacent property was made into a recreation ground.

The new site succeeded in attracting business and had to be enlarged in 1933. Its character changed in the 1950s, when new regulations ensured that dairy cows were tuberculin tested. Holmfirth was then the nearest attested market and Penistone became essentially a venue for fat-stock. Since 1994 the market site has been put to further use. As well as the regular Thursday market, sheep, pigs and cattle are sold on Mondays, and store cattle and pigs are sold on Saturdays. A thriving general sales area adjoining the present-day cattle market offers a wide variety of articles and produce.[25] Three hundred years after its foundation, Penistone market continues to thrive.

The Grammar School
Old photographs and prints of the centre of Penistone show that the

centre of the town was dominated by three buildings: the church, the cloth hall, and the grammar school that had been founded in 1392 and rebuilt in 1716. An Inquisition of 1604 into the endowments of the school[26] was told that many of the old deeds were lost or illegible. One that survived was produced to show that in 1392 Thomas Clarel, the absentee lord of Penistone, granted to John del Rhodes and others a piece of land in the Kirk Flatt, 'so much as extends and lies between five stones placed as bounds'. The new owners of this property were also given the usual common right to dig peat for fuel on the moors. The deed did not mention a school, but clearly referred to the site on which the building was erected. Clarel was still remembered in 1604 as the founder of the school. The group of people who accompanied John del Rhodes may well have been the first governors.

The school stood in Kirk Flatt until its removal to its present site at Weirfield in 1893. It lay close to the northern side of the church – the 'kirk' – at the top of Church Hill. Many an early school was founded in or just beyond a churchyard, for the first masters were normally priests, often those who served a chantry chapel. Perhaps the priest of the chantry of St Mary followed contemporary practice elsewhere in supplementing his income by teaching? A continuous history cannot be proved with certainty, but in 1443, half a century after its foundation, the 'Free Grammar School of Penistone' received a bequest in the will of William Turton of Denby.[27] The medieval origins of the school are proved beyond doubt by this will.

The abolition of chantries by Edward VI in 1547 and the confiscation of their lands affected educational provision throughout the country, but in common with many other places the people of Penistone seem to have preserved the endowments of their chantry chapels for the use of their school. The rents of cottages and gardens that had once supported the chantry priests now paid the wages of the schoolmaster. In 1630 a survey, valuation and rental of lands belonging to 'the Free Grammar School at Peniston' recorded property in the East Field, St Mary's Lane, Castle Green, Hackings, the Town Green, Lumbroyd, the Hermit Yard, St John's Chapel and the field known as Rudbroom.[28] The names of several masters during the seventeenth century are known to us, starting with Mr Hey in 1613 and including that of Nathan Staniforth, the puritan clergyman who had been ejected from his Derbyshire vicarage in 1662. Penistone was still a puritan stronghold and the parishioners were pleased to get such an able man as their master. He taught on average about sixty boys, the most famous of whom was Nicholas

A Biltcliffe photograph of Penistone Grammar School, rebuilt in 1716 on the site that it had occupied since 1392.

Saunderson of Thurlstone, the blind boy who became Lucasian Professor of Mathematics at the University of Cambridge.

The successful establishment of a weekly market and annual summer fair in 1699 transformed Penistone from a village into a small town and encouraged the leading families to reorganise and rebuild the school so as to accommodate boarders. In 1702 John Ramsden of Batley was appointed master to teach 'all the rudiments of the Latin and Greek Tongues, with the Rhetoric' to the 'Grammar Scholars' and English and Latin to 'the poorer sort'. Ramsden promised not to allow

> *any more play-days or Holy-days than are commonly allowed in the Best Governed Schools in this Kingdom*

and to

> *carefully endeavour by moderate correction and other provident methods to restrain all swearing, cursing, lying, and other evil practices, spoken or committed within or without the School by any under his Authority.*

He was also obliged to give weekly instruction in the church catechism. The rebuilding of the school was completed in 1716. This is the building that appears in old photographs and prints and which remained in use until 1893.

The school had fifty boys in 1743 and forty boys in 1764. An advertisement for a new master in 1785 asked for someone 'properly qualified to teach Latin and Greek Classics, Writing, Accounts and the Higher Branches of Mathematics'. The following year, the new appointee, Jonathan Wood, advertised

> *a very pleasant and convenient house where Youth may be genteely boarded and educated in Classical and Mathematical learning for thirteen guineas per annum. Entrance Ten Shillings and Sixpence. Young Gentlemen not boarded at the house may be taught Reading, Writing and English Grammar for Five Shillings and Sixpence per quarter.*

Arithmetic and Languages cost another two shillings. Wood's early promise was not sustained and by 1827 he was teaching only at the elementary level of reading, writing and accounts.

The school continued to provide an elementary rather than a grammar school education for much of the nineteenth century. A government report of 1884 noted that only a few of the sixty-two boys were above elementary age. The school was not in a good shape in 1892 when Joseph Fulford was appointed headmaster, a position which he retained until 1921. During his time the school changed fundamentally, though it continued to take boarders until his

The original block of the present Penistone Grammar School, completed in 1911.

retirement. In 1893 a major decision was taken to abandon the old site in Kirk Flatt, which had been used for five hundred years, and to move the school out of town to Weirfield. A new block was completed by 1911. Another revolutionary change was the admittance of girls in 1907. Fulford deserves to be remembered not just for overseeing these changes but as an outstanding headmaster who raised standards to a new high level.

When Fulford retired the school had 258 pupils, only four of whom were sixth formers. His successors, G W Morris (1921-28) and E F Bowman (1928-58), expanded the sixth form in the 1920s and 1930s and encouraged pupils to go on to university or teacher training college. At that time, admission was by the payment of fees or by scholarship. The school served a wide catchment area, extending to the Dearne valley villages in the north and to Stocksbridge, Deepcar, Oughtibridge and Wharncliffe Side in the south. Only a small minority of pupils came from Penistone. Under Bowman the school began to enjoy an academic reputation. The emphasis was on examination work, with a house system for competitive sport and a prefect system and cadet force to instil a sense of responsibility and discipline. When I was a pupil from 1949 to 1956 the school seemed a traditional institution with a long history, but I can now see that its character was different both before and after Bowman's thirty years. I was an early beneficiary of the 1944 *Education Act*, which made it possible for working-class children to attend grammar school and go on to university. When 'the Boss', as we all called Mr Bowman, wrote a supporting reference for my application to university, he urged the interviewing committee to make allowance for the fact that I was 'rather a roughly spoken lad'.

The school has altered considerably over the centuries, but the most far-reaching changes have been in modern times. It is now a very different institution from the one that was founded in 1392, but then all ancient establishments celebrate their long histories even though they have changed out of all recognition with the passage of time.

Chapter Seven

Highways and Byways

✠

The pattern of the ancient highways and byways of Penistone parish is still evident on the ground. Some of the oldest roads continue in use, pounded by heavy modern traffic, while others are overgrown with shrubs, brambles and rosebay willow herb but can be followed by the use of maps, place-names and surviving features in the landscape, such as holloways, causeys, packhorse bridges and eighteenth century guide stoops. The villages, hamlets and farmsteads of the outlying townships were connected to the parish church and, later, to the market alongside it by recognised routes known as church ways or kirk gates. The kirkgate from Carlecoates to Penistone was mentioned in an arbitration award of the 1570s and

The causey from Gunthwaite to Penistone, shown here on the stretch between Cat Hill and Well House.

disputed common land at Snowden Hill in 1602 was bounded by the church way.[1] Gunthwaite was linked to Peniston by a flagged path, or causey, which descends the hillside from the Bosvilles' hall and barn alongside a deep, overgrown holloway that once served as a cart track. Beyond the mill dam in the valley bottom the route climbs to the seventeenth century Cat Hill Hall and continues towards Well House as a paved horse and foot path, the finest to survive in the Penistone district. Another narrow path that is confined between two walls as it comes over Stottercliffe was probably once a similar causey that linked Thurlstone and Penistone. A third path from Top o' th' Town, Thurlstone, to Ingbirchworth via The Folly is also marked by a few flagstones, but it is now difficult to find the flags that could once be seen on the route that climbed from Midhopestones up Judd Field Lane towards Cubley before Mortimer's Road chose a less difficult ascent past Sheephouse Farm in the 1770s. The antiquity of some other minor routes in the parish is suggested by their names. Cut Gate was dug out of the moss to provide a route from the Derwent valley over the moors to Langsett and Boggard Lane was thought to be haunted. But names can mislead. Boulder Bridge, which spans the River Don near Spring Vale, was mentioned in the will of William Wordsworth, vicar of Penistone, in 1495, but the present stone structure is eighteenth century in style. It has replaced a wooden bridge that took its name from the many boulders in the river bed at that point.

From Elizabethan times responsibility for the maintenance of the local highways and byways lay with the parish or with one or more of its sub-divisions. Each year a local man was elected to serve as overseer of the highways and every householder had to work up to six days under his supervision. Adam Eyre of Hazlehead Hall referred to this practice in his diary in 1647. On 30 May he wrote,

This morne I went to Peniston, to church, on foote, and writ a note for Fr. Haigh, to be read in the church, for mending the way to Denby bridge.

On 22 October that year he noted that an ox of Edward Mitchell's had died in an accident, 'in coming from the common day works, vzt from leading stone to Denby bridge'.[2] This is the bridge that crossed the Don on the way from Penistone or Thurlstone to Denby, at what is now known as Bridge End.

From 1733 the overseers of the highways were directed by the West Riding Justices of the Peace to erect sturdy stone posts, known as guide stoops, to mark directions at remote crossroads, 'where

A guide stoop near Hartcliff Tower. Moved and re-used as a gatepost, it points the way to Penistone, Rotherham and Barnsley. As it records miles, it must have been first erected in 1738.

intelligence is difficult to be had'. Five years later, the JPs ordered that in future, miles should be inscribed on new stoops.[3] A simple guide stoop at Upper Cudworth conforms to this order with the inscription: 'Peniston Road 8m/Wakfield 6m, 1738'. Another stoop that was erected shortly after this new order now serves as a gate post leading towards Hartcliff tower. Its original position is uncertain since the local landscape was transformed by the enclosure of the commons in 1816, but it has not been moved very far. The inscriptions on three sides of the stoop read: 'Penistone 2

Miles/Rotharam [1]2 Miles/Bar[n]sley 8 M[ile]s', yet a turnpike milestone a few hundred yards away marks fifteen miles to Rotherham. The discrepancy in the mileage results from the turnpike authorities using the statutory mile of 1,760 yards while the overseers of the highways used the old customary Yorkshire mile of about 2,200 yards on the guide stoop.

A unique six-sided guide stoop at Dyson Cote in the township of Hunshelf was erected in 1734, before the order to number the miles was made. Unlike the stoop near Hartcliff tower, it does not have fingers pointing the directions, but the traveller used the same principle of turning right from the inscription. The side that reads: 'Barnsley & Pontefract 1734 Doncaster' directs us down to Oxspring bridge, then up Bower Lane to Coates and Keresforth. The next side shows the way to 'Wakefield & Leeds' via the back lane of Roughbirchworth, Willow Bridge and the former *Packhorse Inn* on

A guide stoop at Dyson Cote, erected in 1734. This stoop is unique in having six sides. The traveller turned right from the inscription.

the road to Cawthorne from Silkstone. The enclosure of the surrounding commons has obscured the line of the road that began as a short holloway towards 'Penistone Huthersfield & Hallifax', but the other routes that are marked on the stoop are still in use. The highway that came from Cheshire and Lancashire via 'Woodhead/Motram' continued along the ridge through Hunshelf towards 'Sheffield & Rotterham', while that marked 'Underbank/Bradfield' is a forgotten highway which can be traced all the way from Bradfield and Bolsterstone, as it climbs the crests of several hills and descends steeply into the river valleys. Beyond the Dyson Cote stoop it headed for Willow Bridge and Wakefield. This route was never important enough to be made into a turnpike road and so its old bridges were not widened to allow wheeled vehicles to pass. Many of its old features survive. A guide stoop that stands by Green Farm, on the hills south-west of Stocksbridge, is inscribed 'Uden/Peniston/Bolster-stone'. Half a mile further on, at the junction of Oaks Lane, Machin Lane and Clay Pits Lane, a smaller stoop directed the traveller towards 'Un-sliven-bridge/Middop/Green'. As neither of these stoops records miles, they must have been erected between 1733 and 1738. The likelihood is that they date from 1734, the same year as the Dyson Cote stoop and the packhorse bridge on the same route, which was removed to Glen Howe Park at Wharncliffe Side when Ewden reservoir was constructed. This characteristic packhorse bridge once crossed the Ewden Beck under the name of the New Mill Bridge. In 1734 Benjamin Milnes, a local mason, demolished the old wooden structure and built a sturdier one in stone. Unsliven bridge was another wooden bridge that was replaced in stone about this time, but it was widened in 1796 to take wheeled vehicles as well as packhorses. Willow Bridge is undated but almost certainly dates from about 1734, when all these improvements were made to this old highway from Bradfield to Wakefield. This bridge is a typically rugged yet graceful feature of the packhorse era immediately before the age of turnpike roads.

Several other guide stoops mark another forgotten highway, the old ridgeway from Penistone and Thurlstone to Holmfirth, Meltham and Marsden, which Thomas Jeffreys depicted on his map of Yorkshire in 1772. This highway failed to attract the attention of a turnpike trust. It owes much of its present appearance to the work of the various enclosure commissioners, particularly those who enclosed the commons and wastes of Thurlstone township between 1812 and 1816. West of Thurlstone the road follows a straight line between walls that were built thirty feet apart. A battered stoop that is now set

Willow Bridge. This elegant structure probably dates from 1734, when other improvements were made to the cross-country route from Bradfield to Wakefield.

in one of these walls on the continuation of the route up High Bank to Royd Moor reads: 'Holmfirth 4 mile/Hudde[rs]fiel[d] 8 [mile]/Penistone [2] mile'. The highway clung to the ridge, or sought shelter just below it, as far as Maythorn, then descended steeply to Foster Place and Hepworth, before continuing along Sandy Gate to Holmfirth. Further stoops at Netherthong, Thick Hollins and Meltham all marked the way from Penistone. [4]

The enclosure awards that were made for the various townships of Penistone parish in the first three decades of the nineteenth century each laid out public carriage ways to standard widths. Main routes, such as Mortimer's Road and Cranberry Farm Lane, were made thirty feet wide, but the private carriage and public bridle roads varied in width from twelve to twenty-four feet. Many of the public roads that were authorised by the enclosure commissioners were said to be 'ancient lanes' that had been straightened and defined by new walls. Even some of the turnpike roads were improved in this manner.

The Road over Saltersbrook

The most important ancient highway through the parish of Penistone was that which came from Cheshire and Lancashire up the Longdendale valley via Woodhead and over the county boundary at Saltersbrook. This ancient and natural crossing of the Pennines had been used from time immemorial by teams of packhorses bringing salt from the Cheshire 'wiches' – Northwich, Middlewich and Nantwich – to the market towns of the West Riding. Since at least Roman times salt had been an essential item in every household in the land, for it was used not just to flavour food but to preserve it. Until 1974 Cheshire had an unusual shape, with a long neck in its north-eastern corner, so important was this saltway to the county's economy. Salter names are dotted about the present landscape or can be found on old maps along the routes to the market towns. The Salter Gate that headed from Saltersbrook towards Wakefield formed the northern boundary of Thurlstone township; Salter Hill still marks the ridgeway towards Rotherham as it passes through the township of Hunshelf towards Green Moor and Wortley Forge. Beyond the parish, salter names at Mortomley, Thorpe Hesley and Kimberworth identify the continuation of the route to Rotherham's medieval bridge and market, while similar names at Dodworth, Goldthorpe and Scawsby identify the saltway to Barnsley and Doncaster.[5]

The salters were the most distinctive traders who used this old highway, but they were not the only ones. In 1723 it was claimed that the route over Saltersbrook was 'the more passable way than the moor towards Sheffield', i.e. the Winnats Pass route through Castleton and north Derbyshire.[6] Seventeen years later a petition presented to the House of Commons maintained that this great highway over Saltersbrook was 'most convenient for conveying of goods from the eastern to the western seas'.[7] It was the first road in south-west Yorkshire to be improved by the creation of a turnpike trust that was empowered to charge tolls. In 1732 the section on the Cheshire side of the Pennines was turnpiked as 'the direct way to Black Barnsley'. John Hobson, the Dodworth Green diarist, noted on 5 July 1732 that, 'On Munday last a turnpike was set up at Woodhead, for repairing the rodes betwixt Manchester and Saltersbrooke'. Steps were then taken to improve the Yorkshire section and on 7 November 1735 representatives from Doncaster and Barnsley met to discuss the best procedure.[8] Nearly six years were to pass, however, before an Act was obtained.

The petition presented to the House of Commons by the inhabitants of Doncaster and Barnsley on 19 December 1740 claimed that whereas the Manchester-Saltersbrook road was very well repaired, the Saltersbrook-Doncaster road was 'excessive bad and is now dangerous'.[9] Six miles of moor and heath separated Saltersbrook from Penistone and the rest of the journey was along a road that had been made ruinous by 'many heavy carriages' on their way to Doncaster, whence goods were taken by river and sea to London and foreign parts. The House of Commons committee that examined the bill reported that the road 'is now, and has been, for several years past, in a very ruinous condition'. They found that 'great quantities of manufactured goods, cheese, salt, and potatoes, are carried from Manchester, Barnsley, and parts adjacent, to Doncaster, on horses, and return loaded with hemp, flax, and German yarn' and that the trade could be carried on much easier 'in waggons, carts, etc.'.[10] The yarn which came in great vats could thus be carried more conveniently and exporters could bale their goods at home instead of sending them in packs to London.

The original bill dealt only with the route from Saltersbrook to Barnsley and Doncaster, but on 13 January 1741 the House of Commons received a petition from 'several gentlemen, tradesmen and others' asking for the Rotherham road over Hartcliff Hill to be included.[11] The petitioners made the usual claim that 'the said road by reason of the deepness of the soil, and many heavy loads carried and drawn through the same, is become so founderous in the winter season, that it is dangerous to passengers'. An improved road would be timely because the River Don had just been made navigable as far inland as Rotherham and so heavy, bulky goods could be taken the rest of their journey more cheaply by water. The House of Commons committee accepted these arguments and noted that in its later stages the road would 'greatly facilitate the conveyance of manufactured iron from the forges at Wortley to Rotherham, for the further convenience of water-carriage'.[12]

The Act that was passed in 1741 allowed free passage for stones and gravel necessary for the repair of highways, hay, corn and straw being taken to farms or barns, all farm equipment, lime and manure, also for those travelling to church or chapel, the post mail, soldiers, and horses ridden by the driver of a team of packhorses or of a waggon or cart. The last provision was repealed in 1762 because of many frauds.[13] Half tolls were charged on carts carrying coal or corn, also on cart loads of wood, timber or bark on the Rotherham-Hartcliff Hill section. The Act also ordered that stones or posts should be erected alongside the highway at intervals of one mile. A few of these survive on the branch heading for Rotherham.

The modern road crosses Saltersbrook by a sturdy bridge, constructed in 1828, but the older track followed a higher route from Woodhead, before seeking a lower crossing over an insignificant-looking bridge that has recently been re-built. This bridge was probably erected between 1732 and 1741 and was just wide enough to take wheeled vehicles. After the arduous journey through the Cheshire hills the traveller could rest at *Saltersbrook House*, a former inn that is now a tumble-down ruin by the bridge. Purchased in 1916 by Manchester Corporation Water Works, it was demolished four years later to prevent contamination of the Longdendale reservoirs.[14] The continuation of the highway is plain to see as far as the horizon and the proof that it was more than a local track is supplied by an old milestone lying by the wall near the inn, inscribed 'From [W]ortley XII Miles From Rotherham XXI Miles IWB'.[15] The old route is marked on the modern Ordnance Survey map and compares exactly with the highway that was engraved on maps by Thomas Jeffreys in 1772 and by William Fairbank in 1818.[16] The present detour over the high bridge was not completed until 1828, nearly ninety years after the passing of the Act.[17] Carriages, carts and waggons all followed this ancient route and although the stretch up to and beyond the Lady Cross was improved it is no wonder that James Harrop, the first man to drive a stage-waggon from Manchester to Barnsley and Doncaster, complained that the condition of the road was 'summat scandalous'.[18]

The difficulties in using this Pennine crossing were very real. John Hobson noted in his diary that 13 December 1726

was such an ill day for frost, snow, and wind, that severall people had like to have perished in comming over the moors from Woodhead.[19]

Entries in the Penistone burial registers show that these fears were realistic: '10 March, 1755. Wm. Wordsworth Starv'd to Death on the Moors'; '15 February, 1763. Jos. Charlesworth from Burton lost in Snow', and '6 March, 1764. James Marsh starv'd in the Snow'.[20] A quarter of a mile beyond the Lady Cross a small, rounded stone that is almost hidden in the grass is inscribed XX. Jeffreys's map identifies it as the twentieth milestone from Rotherham. It shows beyond doubt that the original turnpike road followed the old saltway exactly, but that the later road was banked and levelled a few feet away. In 1883-34 road makers were asked to tender for the job of reducing the hill above Boardhill Bar, leading up to Fiddlers Green, and of 'forming, levelling, draining, stoning and finishing the improvement of the road'. Three years later, further tenders were put out to improve the section of the road from Fiddlers Green to Saltersbrook.[21]

Four new inns were erected along this moorland route. The (demolished) *Miller's Arms* stood by the new bridge at Saltersbrook and was a regular meeting place of the local Shepherds' Society. The

The Millers' Arms, *Saltersbrook, 1907. Erected alongside the new bridge in 1828, it is shown here at the annual meeting of the Shepherds' Society. It has been demolished and the site cleared.*

former *Plough and Harrow* at Fiddlers Green stood near the crossing of the old and new roads. Further on, the original highway can be traced both on the map and on the ground along the stretch known as the 'Snow Road' from the posts that were set up at either side to mark its course during winter. Three miles from Saltersbrook the track is rejoined by the modern road at the former Boardhill toll bar just above another new inn, *The Dog and Partridge*. The last inn was originally known as the *New Inn* when it was completed in 1827, but then became known as *The Flouch*. An old story that the pub took its name from the landlord having a 'slouch' or hare-lip sounds highly unlikely; a more plausible tale is that it was re-named *The Plough* and that paint peeled off the first and fifth letters, so it acquired its name humorously. A stone milestone a short distance away on the opposite side of the road is inscribed: 'Barnsley 13 Miles Manchester 23 Miles'.

A turnpike milestone near The Flouch, *marking the distances to Barnsley and Manchester.*

Three-quarters of a mile beyond *The Flouch*, the old and the new roads diverged again at Fullshaw Cross. In 1741 the Doncaster-Saltersbrook trustees decided to avoid the old, direct course over Hartcliff Hill and down Hillside by following what had been a minor route that swings sharply left down the valley through Millhouse Green and Thurlstone, rejoining the other track at the bottom of Hornthwaite Bank, just past the Thurlstone corn mill. The Doncaster road then stuck to the line of the old saltway along the present road through Hoylandswaine, Silkstone and Dodworth, past toll bars at Keresforth, near Stairfoot, between Goldthorpe and

The old route from Hartcliff down to Bankside and Homthwaite is now a pleasant track for horse-riders and walkers.

Hickleton, and at Scawsby. All five original toll bars upon this route are marked on Jeffreys's map in 1772 and the whole of the highway from the bottom of Hornthwaite Bank was surveyed by John Warburton in 1718-20, long before it became a turnpike road.[22]

The road from Fullshaw Cross to Rotherham followed the other branch of the saltway over Hartcliff Hill and along the ridge through Hunshelf. Droves of cattle headed the other way, from the market and fairs at Rotherham to the industrial towns of Lancashire and Cheshire. The farmers of Peck Pond and Cranberry took advantage of all this traffic to convert their farmsteads into alehouses. The sixteenth milestone to Rotherham can be found in the wall at Paw Hill in the position marked by Jeffreys; the wall was built around it in 1816 when the commons were enclosed. The fifteenth milestone has in recent years been moved a few yards to a safe position, beyond the junction with the lane leading to Penistone. The only other milestone to survive into modern times was one that stood beyond Kimberworth, which was marked 'To Rotherham 1, Wortley 8 miles'.

The Rotherham-Hartcliff Hill road soon proved a burden to the turnpike trustees. When the Act came up for renewal in 1762 it was admitted that 'notwithstanding the money sunk, and toll collected, it has been found the same has not been effectual, but the said road in many parts continued very bad.'[23] The chief problem was that traffic had been lost to the turnpike road heading out of Lancashire through

The sixteenth milestone to Rotherham at Paw Hill, marked on Jeffreys's map (1772) and built into a wall after the enclosure award of 1816. The Ordnance Survey added their bench mark later.

Wakefield to Doncaster and to the new Sheffield to Buxton or Chapel-en-le-Frith road, 'so that little Toll can now be collected'. Only one toll bar, at Kimberworth, had been erected and ninety per cent of the local rates that had been raised to improve the highways and byways had gone on this road. Petitioners claimed that it was necessary to increase the tolls or to have

> *a catch penny made of the coals and other things that pass half a mile or a mile upon the said road, which generally are led in summer, when the roads are naturally good.*

However, some powerful landlords had a vested interest in conveying coal as cheaply as possible, so this suggestion was not taken up. A House of Commons committee was told on 17 March 1767 that the turnpike trust was £1,000 in debt and that the tolls were insufficient to pay the interest. Saintforth Wroe, the surveyor, thought that if the road were repaired more carriages and travellers would make use of it. He claimed that 'land carriage is cheaper on this road than on any road in England'.[24] Thomas Jeffreys's map did not mark any toll bars at all between Hartcliff Hill and Rotherham. The *Turnpike Act* was finally renewed in 1767, but when the powers needed fresh approval twenty-one years later the section from Fullshaw Cross to Wortley crossroads was abandoned. It was left to the enclosure commissioners a generation or so later to widen and straighten the western section of the highway as it passed through Penistone parish.

Mortimer's Road

Another ancient moorland highway that crossed Penistone parish became known as Mortimer's Road after Hans Winthrop Mortimer, Lord of Bamford, Member of Parliament and the owner of large estates in Essex, Derbyshire and London.[25] He was instrumental in obtaining an Act in 1771

> *For repairing and widening the road leading from Penistone Bridge through Bamford to join the turnpike road between Hope and Sheffield near Mytham Bridge and also from Hathersage to Grindleford Bridge and the roads severally leading from Bamford Woodgate over Yorkshire Bridge to the guide post on Thornhill Moor to or near the Eighth Milestone on Hathersage Moor and to the village of Derwent in the County of Derby.*

Just before the improvements were carried out, Thomas Jeffreys's map of Yorkshire marked the route simply as a 'Bridle Way', but the new bridges that were constructed in 1775-76 made it passable for wheeled traffic. John Wilson, the antiquary of Broomhead Hall, wrote in his notebook on 26 August 1776 that

> *Mr Francis Scott, Grace Scott & Mrs Armitage came here down Uden from Wakefield by Bullhouse, being the first chaise that ever came that way.*[26]

The turnpike trustees were responsible for improving the highway between Penistone and Grindleford, where it joined the roads from Sheffield to Buxton and from Grindleford to Calver and Bakewell, both of which had been turnpiked in 1758. The toll house that was erected in 1758 still stands by Grindleford Bridge. Mortimer's Road, as it quickly became known, went via Leadmill Bridge (by *The Plough*) into Hathersage, then along Jaggers' Lane (named after the packmen who took lead from the mines to the smelting mills) to the Marquis of Granby and Mytham Bridge, before turning past Bamford Mill towards Yorkshire Bridge and the former village of Ashopton (which now lies under the reservoir). The ruins of an old bridge to the east of the reservoir mark the crossing of Ladybower Beck. The Snake Pass, which cuts across Mortimer's Road at this

This re-erected guide stoop at Moscar has been badly damaged, but we can just make out that it marked the ways to Penistone and Hope in 1737.

point, was not constructed until 1818-21, so Mortimer's Road originally went north of the *Ladybower Inn* towards Moscar, over unenclosed moorland, along what is now a public footpath. A guide stoop that was erected in 1737 to show the ways to Penistone, Hope and Sheffield, was later mutilated by a gamekeeper to deter ramblers, but it was found in 1998 and re-erected 220 yards south west of Moscar House Farm, close to its original position.

Claims on signboards that the *Strines Inn* dates back to the thirteenth century are nonsense. It was not there when Thomas Jeffreys published his map of Yorkshire in 1772. John Wilson of Broomhead Hall noted that in 1776 'Anthony Worrall set up the sign of the Bull at Strynds and sold ale' .[27] Strines is a dialect word for a stream or a narrow river crossing. The wooden bridge over the stream below the hill was replaced by the present Strines Bridge in 1775. An extra horse had to be provided to haul vehicles up the steep ascent from the bridge, as far as the 'Take Off' stone opposite the inn. After crossing another new bridge at Agden, the road climbs past Mortimer House towards Ewden. A stone on the lane between High Bradfield and the Strines route was erected in 1753 to guide travellers to Penistone, Bradfield and Sheffield. At the junction of this lane and Mortimer's Road another stoop is inscribed: 'Peniston Rd 5M/ Sheffield R 7M/Bradfield R 2M 1740/Hope R 9M'. The road then descends past Broomhead Hall to the bridge over the Ewden Beck, which was built about 1776, after which the traveller was faced with a steep climb of 1-in-4 with a kink in the road to help the tiring horses; the old packhorse track had gone straight up the hillside. Mortimer's Road then descended to Midhopestones before another steep climb past Sheephouse Farm as far as a second 'Take Off' stone at the top of the hill.[28] The old packhorse track had gone straight up Judd Field Lane and over the ridge to Cubley. The new course is still known as Mortimer Road on its descent to Penistone, where it met the Sheffield to Halifax turnpike road of 1777. Mortimer hoped to provide a profitable link between the industrial districts of north Derbyshire and the West Riding, but this proved to be one of several of his ventures that failed and he died in bankruptcy in 1807. Turnpike trusts had to renew their authority every twenty-one years. The Act for Mortimer's Road was renewed in 1792, but not in 1813. It did not have a long life as a turnpike road.

The Sheffield to Halifax road
Much more successful was the Sheffield to Halifax turnpike road of 1777. This ancient highway had been marked on John Warburton's map of Yorkshire in 1718-20, long before the turnpike era, together with the road from Saltersbrook to Doncaster. It was clearly considered an important route. The road left Sheffield via Wadsley Bridge, Fox Hill, Grenoside and the ridgeway through Wharncliffe Chase to Wortley. A milestone at the junction with Bank Lane, near Cundy Houses in the former chase, is inscribed: 'Manchester 26 Miles/Sheffield 7 Miles/Hudersfield 15 Miles/Rotheram 8 Miles'. Fifty years after the passing of the *Turnpike Act*, a new route from

The Travellers' Inn *at Four Lane Ends on the Sheffield-Halifax turnpike road of* 1777.

Wadsley Bridge was constructed along 'Halifax Road' to the *Crown Inn* and Wortley, by-passing the old part of Grenoside village and Wharncliffe Chase. After zig-zagging round the church at Wortley the road followed the ridge to Thurgoland, Hoylandswaine Heights and Ingbirchworth, a route that was widened and much improved in the 1930s. On reaching the *Traveller's Inn* at Four Lane Ends a different option was to descend Bower Hill and head for Penistone up Church Hill, where a stone milestone that is inscribed 'Sheffield 13 Miles' is set into the lower end of the churchyard wall. It may well date from 1777, when the road was turnpiked.

In his survey, Warburton noted that from Penistone the road crossed the River Don at Bridge End by a stone bridge of two arches.[29] A milestone that is fixed in the wall by Netherfield Chapel is marked 'London 1777, Huddersfield 12½, Penistone ½'. The turnpike road then followed the old track along the present course through Ingbirchworth and Shepley. A guide stoop in the Tolson museum at Huddersfield, which stood originally at Shelley Bank Bottom, bears the inscription: 'Huddersfield Miles [5]/Wakefield Miles 12/ Penistone 1758 Sheffield Miles [2?.]' and a guide stoop at Farnley Moor End, which is inscribed on three sides with pointing fingers, reads: 'Huddersfield 3 Miels/Pennystone 6 Miles Holmfirth

2 Miles /Jon. Hoyle Constable Thos. Bothomley Surveyor 1738'. On the Penistone side, 'Honley 2 Miles' was added later in a different style of lettering and hand symbol. The road then climbed up to Almondbury, instead of following the modern route along the valley via Waterloo, into Huddersfield and so on to Halifax.

New turnpike roads

The three turnpike roads that have been followed so far stuck to old highways, with minor diversions. Entirely new routes were not created in South Yorkshire until the early years of the nineteenth century. The first was the Wadsley to Langsett turnpike road of 1805, so called because it left the Sheffield to Halifax road at Wadsley Bridge and joined the Saltersbrook to Doncaster and Rotherham road at the *Flouch Inn* at the edge of Langsett township. In 1821 this road was extended through Hazlehead and Crowedge towards Huddersfield. Old highways had avoided river valleys but the new Wadsley to Langsett turnpike road followed the course of the Don and Little Don closely. Its link with Sheffield was a major incentive for Samuel Fox to build his works and an entirely new settlement at Stocksbridge. Before the new road was built, travellers had to use winding lanes that came over the hills.

New inns soon provided refreshment alongside the turnpike road. Across the Little Don from Midhopestones, just inside Penistone parish, William Payne, lord of Langsett since 1802, built a handsome inn that also catered for those who used the Strines route. Known as the *Rose and Crown*, it closed in 1878 but it survives as a building. Payne also built the *Waggon and Horses* at Langsett and the present Sheephouse Farm. In his *Tour of the Don* (1837), John Holland recounts his vivid impression of the *Rose and Crown*:

> When a person enters the inn, at which the coaches stop at Midhope Stones, the first thing that strikes his eye, especially if he is hungry, is a sort of rack suspended on the joists of the ceiling of the kitchen, and overlaid with some scores of thin oat-cakes, or, as the batch is called, reed bread; having been placed on the rails of the rack in its flaccid state, the manner in which each cake is warped, first by hanging over the edges, and secondly by drying, gives it a curious appearance to a stranger. When eaten, it is found to be just so tenderly crisp, and withal so sweet, added to its undoubted wholesomeness, that many persons are extremely fond of it.[30]

The last turnpike road to be constructed through part of Penistone parish was that which was authorised in 1825 as the Barnsley to Shepley Lane Head road and which was completed in 1830. Now the

A cast iron tutrnpike milestone on the Barnsley to Shepley Lane Head road of 1825, marking the way to Cawthorne and Denby Dale.

A635, it came via Cawthorne and Nether End and joined the Sheffield to Halifax turnpike road at the *Sovereign Inn*. It ceased to be a turnpike road in 1875,[31] but, together with the A636 from Denby Dale to Wakefield and the Penistone to Huddersfield railway line, it catered from the growing textile trade along the Dearne valley in the middle decades of the nineteenth century.

Once the major highways were made into turnpike roads, regular coaching services came through Penistone. In 1822 Baines's *West Riding Directory* noted three coaches a week: to Sheffield and to Huddersfield and Halifax. Letters were taken to Wakefield and so on to other places on Mondays, Thursdays and Saturdays. The success of the turnpike roads encouraged the building of new inns, such as *The Waggon and Horses* at Oxspring and the *Dunkirk* at Lower Denby, and the conversion of old farmhouses into alehouses. For example, Jockey House on the road from Thurgoland to Hoylandswaine Heights was formerly a pub known on the 1826 enclosure award as *The Horse and Jockey*. But the triumph of the coaching era was short-lived. By the middle of the nineteenth century it was quicker and cheaper to travel on the railways.

Chapter Eight

Industrial Change

✠

The nineteenth century was the period of the most dramatic changes in the long history of Penistone parish. In the first quarter of the century the countryside was transformed by the division of the commons and wastes into the rectangular, stone-walled fields that are such a striking feature of the landscape when viewed from the top road

from Thurgoland to Ingbirchworth. At the same time, new textile mills along the banks of the Don and the Dearne were changing the local economy and attracting new settlements alongside them. Then in the middle years of the century came the railways and the steelworks at Stocksbridge and Spring Vale. The population figures for each of the eight townships of Penistone parish in the various census returns show how numbers grew, in line with national trends, from 3,681 in 1801 to 11,160 a hundred years later. By the end of Victoria's reign, the parish of Penistone had three times as many people living within its boundaries than it had at the beginning of the nineteenth century. Meanwhile, the main branches of the old leading families – the Bosvilles, Burdetts, Wordsworths, Riches and Micklethwaites – had disappeared. Their places were taken by men who made their money out of industry.

High Street, Penistone. The narrow main street captured by Joshua Biltcliffe in the horse-and-cart era.

Table 8.1 – Population figures for Penistone parish, 1801-1901

Township	1801	1811	1821	1831	1841	1851	1861	1871	1881	1891	1901
Denby	1061	1132	1412	1295	1690	1709	1813	1637	1559	1661	1765
Gunthwaite	111	119	86	99	66	77	81	83	70	68	57
Hunshelf	327	429	436	531	578	729	1150	1283	1404	1559	1680
Ingbirchworth	170	264	367	371	419	393	368	303	335	321	274
Langsett	204	235	325	320	303	296	280	246	271	263	922
Oxspring	219	255	247	283	241	278	346	370	350	322	397
Penistone	493	515	645	703	738	802	860	1549	2254	2553	3073
Thurlstone	1096	1282	1524	1599	1872	2018	2251	2639	2851	2735	2992
Parish total	**3681**	**4231**	**5042**	**5201**	**5907**	**6302**	**7149**	**8110**	**9094**	**9482**	**11160**

We need to note that the figures for Thurlstone township in 1841 were inflated by the 225 railway navvies who were working at the Dunford Bridge end of the Woodhead tunnel and that the figures for Langsett township in 1901 included men who were constructing the reservoir. Nevertheless, the trends are clear. At the beginning of the nineteenth century, Thurlstone and Denby were the most populous townships in the parish because of employment opportunities in the textile trades. As their mills were enlarged, the population of both townships continued to grow, despite some difficulties in the mid-Victorian period. The rise of the population of Hunshelf and Penistone townships came later, after Samuel Fox founded his works at Stocksbridge, on the Hunshelf township boundary, and the Yorkshire Steel & Iron Works began production at the eastern end of Penistone township. By 1901, for the first time in its history, Penistone township was the most populous in the parish. The steady decline of the population of Gunthwaite township while that of its neighbours was rising made the contrast between the industrial and rural parts of the parish even more pronounced.

Male occupations in 1806

In 1806, at the height of the Napoleonic Wars, nearly all the men aged between 18 and 45 who lived in the forty townships of Staincross wapentake were listed as being liable for militia service.[1] The lists are an invaluable local record, for they note the men's occupations and thus show how different the employment structures of the various townships within Penistone parish had become by the beginning of the nineteenth century. The great industrial changes that were to have such an effect on life in the neighbourhood had just begun.

Table 8.2. Occupations in the militia returns of 1806

Occupation	Denby	Gunthw.	Hunshelf	Ingbirch.	Langsett	Oxspring	Penistone	Thurlstone
Weaver	63	4		7		1	7	40
Clothier	12	3	11	1	1	4	1	21
Cloth dresser	1						2	4
Cotton spinner	1							
Slubber	1							1
Dyer	1							1
Yarn maker								1
Tailor	2						1	3
Hatter							1	
Roper								1
Oil presser								1
Merchant								1
Book keeper								1
Millwright								2
Miller		2						1
Yeoman						3		3
Farmer	8	2	5	1	12	4	1	1
Butcher	2						2	4
Tanner	6						2	
Fellmonger						1		
Skinner						3		
Chandler								2
Dry salter	1							
Grocer							1	
Mercer							1	
Apothecary							1	
Carpenter			2	2	1		3	1
Joiner						2	3	
Cooper							1	1
Shoemaker	4	1	2	2	1	2	1	3
Saddler							1	
Ostler							1	
Gardener		1						1
Paper maker								4
Clogger							1	
Collier		2						3
Mason			2				14	6
Smith				1	1		2	
Blacksmith			2			1		4
Nailer				3		2		
Wire drawer			3			2		
Forgeman			2					
Iron roller			5					
Strip weaver			2					
Crapper			1					
Labourer	4	3	15	10	1	12	11	18
Servant	7			7	4	1	1	
Waiter							1	
Preacher								1
Gentleman			1					
Constable	1	1	1			1		1
No occupation		3						

Most striking of all were the large numbers of weavers and clothiers in Thurlstone and Denby townships, especially when compared with the modest numbers recorded elsewhere. Thurlstone had 40 weavers, 21 clothiers, 4 cloth dressers, a slubber, a yarn maker and a dyer; in all, 68 of its 130 men aged between 18 and 45 were employed in the textile trades. Denby had 63 weavers, 12 clothiers, a dyer, a dresser, a slubber and a cotton spinner amongst its 114 men in this age group. Thurlstone and Denby lay at the southern edge of the great West Riding textile district and they were the first townships in Penistone parish to be changed by the Industrial Revolution. Meanwhile, the neighbouring townships in the Dearne valley were being transformed by their new mills. Cumberworth had 91 weavers, 6 clothiers, 3 cutters, 12 tradesmen and only 32 men who were employed in other occupations, while Clayton West had 44 weavers, 6 clothiers, 7 dressers, 2 cutters, 1 cropper and 1 wool comber.

The term 'clothier' had long been used in the West Riding to describe a farmer-weaver whose wife and children helped to produce a piece of cloth each week for the various Piece Halls in the market towns. In the 1806 militia returns the term seems to describe not only small manufacturers but those men who continued to farm a smallholding in addition to weaving cloth. The old farmhouse at Catshaw, with its range of weavers' windows, was typical of this common arrangement. The term 'weaver', on the other hand, was used in the militia returns for a man who worked full-time at his loom in an upstairs chamber. As the population was rising dramatically, fewer men had the opportunity to farm a little land and so weaving became their sole occupation. The trade was expanding rapidly at this time, for weaving was not yet mechanised and more and more cottage looms were needed to cope with the increased production of yarn from the mills.

The preparation and spinning processes became mechanised by water power during the last quarter of the eighteenth century. The old fulling mills, where cloth was scoured and thickened, were often adapted to the extra task of scribbling raw wool into yarn, though sometimes scribbling mills were built anew. At first, the men who built these mills were small employers from 'clothier' backgrounds who supplied local spinners and weavers. The scribbling machines were designed to disentangle the yarn by a series of wire brushes attached to cylinders, which were turned by a water wheel. Another new machine was the slubbing billy, which drew out loose cardings and wound the yarn on to bobbins; its thirty to fifty spindles were worked by a slubber and two or three children who fed the machine and 'pieced' together the strands of yarn. Women and children formed a high proportion of the mill workforce, while the men wove cloth in their cottages. The villages to the south and east of Huddersfield all specialised in fancy weaving, especially the manufacture of waistcoats with decorative floral patterns. This trade began to flourish in the last quarter of the eighteenth century, but during the depression of the late 1820s wages fell to seven or eight shillings a week for the cheapest class of goods. The invention of the 'witch' loom, which was capable of weaving a great variety of patterned cloths, then stimulated the trade to a new level of prosperity. Some small weaving sheds and warehouses eventually become steam-powered weaving mills, but fancy weaving was still performed on handlooms in cottages well into the 1880s.[2]

Denby Dale

In 1806 Denby township was full of weavers and clothiers. By 1851, 134 people found employment there in the fancy weaving trade. It is therefore puzzling that the township does not have the characteristic rows of weavers' cottages lit by rows of upstairs windows that are found in Thurlstone and many other parts of the West Riding textile district. A few simple ones can be seen at Birds Edge, but this type of building is not characteristic of the textile settlements of the

Denby Dyke, the old name for Denby Dale, depicted on Thomas Jeffreys's map of Yorkshire (1772), before the great expansion of the nineteenth century.

Dearne valley. But as many mills were built in isolated positions, the early mill owners had to provide houses for their workers. Numbers 2-10 Dearnside Road, Denby Dale, are good surviving examples which face into the mill yard alongside the owner's house.[3] In 1806 the new village of Denby Dale was only just developing and perhaps had not yet got its name; Thomas Jeffreys's map of 1772 marks the small cluster of houses near the old corn mill as Denby Dyke. Here was one of the several scattered hamlets that characterised the township, set in a lovely, rural valley. The corn mill stood by the Dearne at the bottom of Miller Hill. It was probably the one that had belonged to the Burdetts in 1646 and which was run by Nathaniel Shirt a hundred years later. Baines's *West Riding Directory* of 1822 names Joseph Dalton, corn miller, and Joshua Moxon, miller, so by that time both the Upper and Lower Corn Mills were in business.[4]

Jeffreys's map also marks the mysteriously named Putting Mill, a fulling mill in an isolated position downstream, near where the modern Ordnance Survey map marks Putting Hill.[5] Tom Umpleby has suggested that it may have been the mill that was owned by Ward & Haywood, scribbling millers, who were listed in the 1822 directory (when William Heywood was also recorded as a woollen and cotton manufacturer). Although Lancashire was the great centre of the cotton trade, in the early years of the nineteenth century many places in the West Riding had a cotton mill. Thomas Hartley was the miller here in 1830. It ended its days as a paper mill, where rags were crushed by water power.[6] Brown paper was needed for wrapping finished goods, so each of the new industrial districts needed its own paper mills.

Thomas Jeffreys's map of Yorkshire (1772) marks Birds Edge as a landscape feature without any buildings, but by 1776 a fulling and woollen mill had been erected there. It was fed by a reservoir on the south bank of the upper reaches of the River Dearne and in 1801 it was known as 'William Dickenson's Mill'. Elihu Dickenson, the High Flatts clothier, was also involved.[7] In the middle years of the nineteenth century the site was converted by the Hirst family to the manufacture of fancy woollens and worked by steam power. Some of the mill workers were housed at Birds Edge, alongside the highway from Penistone to Huddersfield, and provided with a school and a United Methodist chapel.

During the closing years of the eighteenth century a fulling and scribbling mill was erected at Hartcliffe, immediately west of the later railway viaduct at Denby Dale. Jeffreys's map shows no buildings in this area in 1772, but by 1804 John Wood, woollen manufacturer, and Nathaniel Shirt, corn miller, had established a mill for scribbling and carding wool and for the spinning of cotton twist. The 1806 militia returns name John Hough, cotton spinner, and Jonathan Stephenson, slubber, who probably worked here. In 1822 *Baines's Directory* noted John Wood & Sons, fancy, woollen and worsted manufacturers of Denby Dale; the firm were amongst the manufacturers of fancy woollen goods who traded in the *White Lion* yard, Huddersfield, every week.[8] In 1850 the site was bought by Zachariah Hinchcliffe & Sons, who greatly expanded Hartcliffe Mills for the spinning of woollen and worsted yarns. This is the only mill in Denby Dale that is still working.

During the middle years of the nineteenth century the original scribbling mills were replaced by much larger factories. Their owners became the leading figures in the new local communities. The three-storey Inkerman Mill on what is now Barnsley Road had belonged to George Pierce, woollen manufacturer. In 1822, but in 1868 it was bought by Brownhill & Scatchard, whose senior partner, John Brownhill of Inkerman House, became a JP. When their Newcomen engine failed to provide adequate power for their weaving machines, the firm moved to Springfield Mill near the river and developed the site on a large scale. Production ceased in 1980, when this complex of buildings was converted into warehouses and shops. The third large mill in Denby Dale was that built by Jonas Kenyon & Sons in 1854. This closed in 1977 and the site is now covered by a housing estate known as Kenyon Bank.[9]

Jeffreys's map of 1772 also marks Cuttlehurst Mill, just across the border in Scissett, and the Scissett fulling and scribbling mill further downstream, but at that time Scissett was just the name of a farm. The Norton family turned Cuttlehurst Mill into a large enterprise and renamed it Nortonthorpe. Out of their considerable profits, they were able to build Bagden Hall and to landscape the surrounding grounds, just inside the Denby township border. By Victorian times, the mill owners had replaced the old rural gentry families as the leaders of local society.

The 1851 census returns, analysed by Chris Heath,[10] record 214 people in Denby township who were directly involved in the textile trades: 102 fancy weavers, 16 fancy waistcoat weavers, 1 fancy manufacturer, 8 fulling millers, 37 bobbin winders, 7 power loom weavers, 7 piercers, 6 cotton dyers, 3 worsted dyers, 1 woollen dyer, 5 slubbers, 3 carders, 3 woollen weavers, 3 warpers, 2 croppers, 2 handloom weavers, 1 woollen engineer, 1 twist winder, 1 winder, 1 warehouse man, 1 pattern weaver, 1 woolcomber, 1 woollen spinner and 1 steam loom weaver.

Denby Dale grew into a Victorian village on both sides of the River Dearne, the stream that acted as the old northern boundary of Denby township. The new settlement pattern was finally recognised in 1895 with the creation of the Denby and Cumberworth Urban District Council. The church at Upper Denby was rebuilt in 1842 and the old chapelry of Denby (which included Gunthwaite and Ingbirchworth) became an independent parish in 1857, but Denby Dale did not get its own church until 1893, when Holy Trinity was constructed in tin; the present stone building was erected in 1939. In the absence of the Established Church, chapels acted as the religious and social centres of the new village. John Wood, the mill owner, held meetings in his textile warehouse at Field House until 1799, when he built the Wesleyan Methodist Chapel and minister's house on the hillside in Cumberworth Lane. Much later, the Victoria Memorial Hall was built on the opposite side of the road as a meeting place and Sunday School; it was demolished in 1977. John Wood's two sons, James and Tedber, emigrated to Australia, but kept their local connections; Tedber led the public subscription for the first Denby Dale school in 1874. The other denominations were the Primitive Methodists, who worshipped in a chapel half way up Miller Hill (which thus got the local name of Ranter Hill), from 1837 to 1962, and the Wesleyan Reform movement, whose Zion chapel on Barnsley Road was erected in 1860, rebuilt in 1908 and closed in 1979. Another Wesleyan Reform chapel, built by a breakaway group in 1911, closed in 1930. The Salvation Army were also present from 1927 to 1970.[11]

The Quaker meeting house in the hamlet of High Flatts near the western edge of Denby township is a much older centre of Nonconformity that was founded in the late seventeenth century by the Jacksons of Totties and Wooldale halls, the Dickensons of High Flatts and other local families. A 1697 datestone survives but the present meeting house dates from the eighteenth century. At the time of Archbishop Herring's visitation of 1743 the Quakers formed the largest group of Dissenters in Yorkshire with 107 meeting houses and about eighty people from nine families attended meetings at High Flatts. Elihu Dickenson, their teacher and occupant of the adjoining farm, died five years later, aged seventy. Another visitation in 1764 reported that Henry Dickenson was the teacher, that about 100 people from eleven parishes attended meetings, and that 'many came out of different parishes'. By 1851 attendance had declined to sixty-one in the morning and an average of twenty in the afternoon during

The eighteenth century Quaker meeting house at High Flatts.

summer time. A minute book of the High Flatts, Wooldale and Lane Head meetings records that £70 had been raised for 'Building the New Meeting house at loomroid near Penistone In the year 1763'. The Lumroyd meeting house was erected at the junction of Chapel Lane and Brockholes Lane, but in 1764 the average attendance was only twenty-five and in 1858 the building was demolished. Some foundations and burial mounds can still to be seen.[12]

Pubs formed a rival attraction, both in the new village of Denby Dale and in the older hamlets. Upper Denby, for instance, had the *Star* (by 1822), the *New Inn* (by 1838) and the *George* (by 1857). And in time, Denby Dale became famous for its monster pies. The story of this tradition has often been told.[13] The first pie was baked in 1788 to mark the recovery from madness of King George III, the second in 1815 to celebrate the defeat of Napoleon at Waterloo. The third pie, upon the repeal of the corn laws in 1846, was the first large one, 7 ft 10ins in diameter and 22 inches deep. It took 10½ hours to bake and was taken in procession to Norman Park, where the event ended in turmoil as the platform on which the pie was displayed collapsed and crowds surged forward. The next pie, baked under the supervision of professional bakers from Halifax in 1887, Queen Victoria's Golden Jubilee year, was an even greater disaster, for the stench when the pie was opened quickly convinced the crowd that it was 'off'. The remains were taken in a mock funeral procession to Toby Wood and buried in quick lime. Another pie was cooked and eaten at Inkerman Mills a week later. The tradition of making enormous pies, each one larger than the last, continued in 1896, 1928, 1964, 1988 and 2000. These have been great occasions for seeing old friends. My parents went to the 1928 event and I have been to each of the last three.

Thurlstone

Thurlstone is the most southerly of the West Riding textile villages, whose mills lie in the river valleys and whose hillsides are dotted with weavers' cottages. These cottages were erected during the early years of the nineteenth century, for the weaving process was not mechanised until a generation or two after the scribbling and spinning mills had begun to turn out great quantities of yarn. Much of the workforce in the mills consisted of women and children, whose menfolk worked at home at their loom. The most striking example of a row of weavers' cottages is at Tenter Hill, whose names comes from the tenter frames in the rear gardens, where cloth was hung to dry after it had returned from the fulling mill and stretched back to its original size by stone weights attached to tenter hooks. The cottages

Tenter Hill, Thurlstone. The best local example of an early nineteenth century row of weavers' cottages.

Plumpton Mill in the Edwardian era. The new church of St Saviour's is seen in the distance.

are three storeys high at the front, two at the back, where the bank slopes steeply, and only one room deep. The top floor, which was well lit by a range of windows, was where the weavers worked at their looms. Internal doors once provided access all the way along. Other examples of smaller ranges of weavers' windows can be found in the village: at the bottom of Rocher, at the beginning of Royd Moor Lane and near Providence Chapel. The cottages at Top o' th' Town, which were built about 1800, housed woollen weavers who made fancy goods, particularly waistcoats. Hand-loom weavers were still recorded in parts of the old village in the census returns of 1881.

About 1803 my great-great-grandfather, John Hey (1781-1855), moved south from Shelley across the parish boundary to live and work as a fancy weaver in one of the new cottages at Top o' th' Town. He was recorded as a weaver in the militia returns and as a fancy weaver when he died in 1855 at the age of seventy-three from 'decay of nature'. He was buried in an unmarked grave in Penistone churchyard. John was the ancestor of all the Heys who now live in Thurlstone, Penistone, Stocksbridge and neighbouring settlements.

The old fulling mill on the River Don, known as the Batty Mill, had been extended into a scribbling, carding, slubbing and fulling mill by 1798. John Camm of Roughbirchworth, the fuller, and James Eyre, the Thurlstone corn, fulling and scribbling miller, each held shares, but much of the finance came from Leeds men, including the famous Gott family of Armley Mill. Vera Nicholson has recently published a full account of this and other mills on the Upper Don.[14] By 1816 it was known as Tomasson's mill, after Thomas Tomasson (1795-1864) came to be tenant. The descendant of a long line of yeomen farmers from Grainfoot, near Ashopton in north Derbyshire, he was recorded as a woollen manufacturer in Baines's *West Riding Directory* in 1822. Five years later he married Catherine Eyre of Plumpton, the heiress of the local milling family. My grandfather, George Hey (1854-1916), worked at Tomasson's, or the Plumpton Cloth Mill, as it was alternatively known, for over twenty years before he moved to Bullhouse as a waggoner at his uncle's corn mill. Plumpton Mill was renowned for the drab livery cloths, spats and gaiters that were made for a wide market, including the royal houses of Europe, and for the thick coverings that were needed for coach seats. The Tomassons carried on the business until it was closed during the depression in 1931. The site was taken over by the extension of Durrans's black lead works five years later.

Vera Nicholson has identified another water mill between the River Don and the goit leading to the corn mill, a site which was known later (and puzzlingly) as Windmill Green.[15] In 1760 George Eyre built four houses here. By 1798 a scribbling mill, worked by a water wheel, and a cropping shop had been erected alongside them. A succession of tenants used it as a woollen mill until the 1870s when George and John Jagger of Thurgoland converted it to a wire mill. When John died in 1884 it became Benjamin Whiteley's rug mill. The building became empty after the Second World War and was demolished in the 1960s.

As we have seen in chapter 3, the old Thurlstone or Hornthwaite corn mill was fed by a long goit from the river into a dam alongside the Manchester Road as it descended to the sharp bend at the bottom of the hill. Alongside it, stood a late eighteenth century Indigo Mill where dyes were made for the woollen cloth industry. It was owned by James Walton (1710-94), descendant of an old local family and the builder of Thurlstone House, but it was worked by tenants. In 1845 William Moorhouse built a cloth and scribbling mill, worked by steam power, next to the dye house and in the 1880s the site was converted into Tinker's Spring Mill Joinery Works.[16] James Walton also owned the oil mill further downstream, which he built in 1761. To extract oil from linseed he no doubt used the products of Zachariah Wainwright's hair cloth and bagging business at Leppings. Zachariah was descended from the yeoman family at

Thurlstone Handbell Ringers, formed in 1855, shown here outside the Thurlstone Sunday school.

Shore Hall and we know something of this unusual small business from letters written by Joseph Wainwright, who emigrated to Pittsburgh with his wife and two young children in 1805 and who continued to write until his death in 1866. The business was run by his relations, Benjamin and John Wainwright of Newhouse and Bankhouse, who seem to have had a monopoly in a fairly wide market.[17]

John Holland wrote in his *Tour of the Don* (1837) that,

> *Thurlstone is a somewhat poor looking and scattered village, or rather hamlet, consisting of stone houses built, for the most part on the left bank of the Don.*

He went on to say that,

> *In the village there are three or four mills, for grinding corn or for other purposes -- and in former years, before canal and railway facilities had so quickened the pace of competition in all kinds of business, considerable quantities of flour were made here. The miller attended the market at Wakefield to purchase grain, which he carried home, ground it into flour and then distributed it to various customers who were scattered, somewhat extensively, about the moors.*[18]

Thurlstone had become a typical West Riding working-class village

Manchester Road, Thurlstone, starting with the Black Bull. *This new part of the village grew up in the first half of the nineteenth century, alongside the textile mills.*

in its appearance, economy and strong Nonconformist tradition. The parish church lay a mile away and, although a Sunday School had been built by public inscription at the north end of the village in

1786, almost another century passed before Church of England
services were held at Town End School; St Saviour's Church at the
west end of Thurlstone was not opened until 1905. Meanwhile, the
chapels had become thriving institutions. In 1786 the
Congregationalists built a chapel at Netherfield, near the eastern
border of the township. The Reverend B Midgley, an Almondbury

clothier, came as preacher and the first seventeen trustees included seven makers of tammy (a good quality cloth), four tailors, three clothiers, a surgeon, a mason, and a joiner. The chapel was greatly enlarged in the 1890s. The Wesleyan Methodists and the Particular Baptists then built places of worship in Thurlstone village. The original Wesleyan Chapel on Work Bank Lane was built in 1793 and was converted into the present house when a new chapel was opened on Manchester Road in 1889. From 1828 the Providence Particular Baptists met in a workshop behind some cottages at Top o' th' Town, near where they built their chapel in 1867. Adult baptisms were performed in a stream and, later, in the River Don. In 1851, 33 people attended the morning service, 37 came in the afternoon and 23 in the evening. The Wesleyan chapel attracted 48 in the morning and 44 in the evening, while the Congregationalists at Netherfield had much larger meetings of 100 in the morning and 120 in the evening; even so, they told the census officers that bad weather had reduced the average attendance by half.[19] The West End Primitive Methodists built a chapel and Sunday School on the Millhouse boundary in 1864 and replaced them fifty years later and old photographs show that large numbers of people, no doubt including many from Millhouse, attended the chapel and Sunday School at Bullhouse. Joseph Bardsley, the long-serving minister there, lived with his wife and two daughters at Moor Royd, within convenient walking distance of the chapel.

Millhouse Green and the western parts of Thurlstone township
The national census that was taken in 1881 reveals a world that was to be familiar to me sixty or seventy years later. Having finished his duties in Thurlstone village, the enumerator walked towards Millhouse and noted the names of the family of William Hoyland, umbrella frame manufacturer, who had recently moved to Paper House and converted the old paper mill to its present use. Hoyland had been born in Sheffield forty-seven years previously, but his six children had all been born in and around Stocksbridge, close to where he had worked with Samuel Fox. Close by at Ecklands Bridge lived Stephen Hallam, a thirty-year old umbrella frame japanner, who had been born at Stockport. The new business had not been going long and was still a small one. A man and eight teenage girls were employed as umbrella makers and two men were described as umbrella rib hardener and umbrella trade tool maker. My mother spent much of her working life here, both before she was married and after the children had grown up. She continued to work at Hoyland's after we had moved to Penistone

Hoyland's Umbrella Works, founded by William Hoyland in 1877 on the site of an eighteenth century paper mill.

in 1949 until her retirement in the 1960s. At that time the wire frames were still being straightened by hand. It would have been hard to find a more old-fashioned, inefficient works. Those of us who remember the place a generation ago are astonished that Hoyland-Fox are now an international leader in the market for umbrellas, operating with the most modern machinery.

The original mill at Millhouse now belonged to William Smith, steel wire manufacturer of nearby Bullhouse Grange. Smith had been born in Thurgoland and perhaps had earlier experience of the trade in the wire mills there. Through the profits of his business, he was able to build a substantial house that now bears the name Bullace Grange, but that is not how it was written originally. Newly-rich Victorians liked to call their houses Grange or Lodge; the owners of Wortley Forge, for instance, built Wortley Grange opposite their works, just inside Hunshelf township, and the Tomassons of Thurlstone lived at Plumpton Lodge. Bullhouse Grange seemed a private, enclosed world to me as a child, though once, on a memorable sultry evening when the midges were biting hard, it was opened for a garden party and cricket on the lawn. In 1881 the five wire drawers and two female wire scourers in Millhouse were no doubt employees of William Smith. The eleven men described as labourers at the steel works, together with the two engine drivers and the night watchman, probably worked at Charles Cammell's at Penistone, a couple of miles away.

Coal mining was a common occupation in the moorland district to the west of Thurlstone at this time. In Millhouse and the surrounding farms and hamlets the census returns record sixty-six men who worked in the local pits. The six-inch Ordnance Survey map of 1854 shows that the thin seam of coal and gannister that stretched along the edge of the Pennines from Sheffield towards Huddersfield was mined not only at Bullhouse but in many 'Old Coal Pits' by Illions and Middle Cliff farms and at Crowedge, where the Hepworth Iron Company would soon open the Sledbrook Colliery. The map also marks two buildings as 'Copperas House'; one just beyond Catshaw Cross and the other by Royd Lane near Millhouse Green. They got their name from the small-scale production of ferrous sulphate for industrial purposes, especially as a mordant for fixing dyes, using the mudstone which was mined between the seams of gannister and coal.[20]

Bullhouse Colliery and some of the smaller pits were owned and managed by John Hinchliffe of Bullhouse Hall. Hinchliffe and his two married sons, who worked at the colliery as book keepers, had been born in Kirkburton, six miles to the north. Their employees included three stationary engine drivers, a banksman and a weighman. The job of one sixteen-year old boy was specified as coal screener. A report into the number of boys between the ages of thirteen and sixteen who were employed in Hinchliffe's pits in 1877 agrees with the evidence of the census returns. The fourteen boys at the Bullhouse pit lived at Green House (2), Robin Row, Knuckle, Bullhouse (2), Copperas, Level Crossing, Rocher, Liley House and Thurlstone (3); the three boys at Middle Cliff pit came from Millhouse (2) and Crowedge; and one Crowedge boy worked in his local mine. Their surnames were the familiar local ones of Barden, Battye, Bramall, Coldwell, Crossland (3), Dransfield, Hinchliffe, Lindley (2), Marsh, Nicholson (2), Penny, Rhodes, Walton and Wilkinson.[21]

In 1881 a Millhouse man and another man from Hartcliff worked as general labourers at a gannister mill and two men at School Wells were gannister grinders. They probably all worked at Bullhouse Colliery. Crowedge had a gannister manufacturer, a gannister merchant, two fireclay workers, several brick makers, an ironstone miner, a tobacco pipe maker, and an earthenware pipe maker. What had recently been an uninhabited area was beginning to take on its present industrial character. The railways also offered opportunities for employment in these wilder western parts. The census enumerators listed three plate layers, three labourers, four signalmen, two station masters, three railway repairers, and a railway official.

The Blacksmith's Arms *at Millhouse, the scene of a murder in 1888.*

Another railway plate layer lived in Millhouse. A few men also worked in the stone quarries in 1881, but their numbers were small compared with those at Thurlstone. Farm labouring was not a common occupation, for the typical hill farm was small and did not need extra hands outside the family, except at harvest time. Sons commonly worked at industrial jobs until they inherited the farm. The distinction between farming and industry was not a sharp one.

All the cottages at Low Millhouse, next to the mill, and nearby on Millhouse Green that I knew as a boy had been erected by 1854. The *Blacksmith's Arms*, which was to be the scene of a tragic murder by a distant member of my family, was there by 1819 and the cottages further along the road to Thurlstone, which were known as Robin Row, had also been erected in the first half of the nineteenth century. In 1886 Harry Hey, the youngest son of my great-grandfather's elder brother, became landlord of the *Blacksmith's Arms*, a decision that was to have dreadful consequences two years later. On the night of 3 September 1888 he wandered from room to room in the pub, with a gun at the ready to fight imaginary enemies. He was suffering from *delirium temens*, for which he had been treated before. At nine o'clock the following morning he shot dead his domestic servant, Margaret Hill, the daughter of a Bullhouse labourer, who was carrying a child and who already had two illegitimate children. He was arrested and taken by train to Barnsley railway station. At court he was said to have been 'jaunty, bright-eyed and with a face flushed with excitement', but later 'sorrowful and stricken'. The court heard that he was normally well-liked, genial and respected as a plasterer and brass band musician, but when he was in drink he was very different. Taking over the pub had not been the best of moves. He had appeared in court earlier on a charge of assaulting his wife, Elizabeth, and a neighbour. Elizabeth had left him on several occasions and on the day of the murder she had run from the pub to hide with neighbours. The case was referred to Leeds Assizes, where the verdict was that he was guilty of wilful murder while in a state of unsound mind. He was detained for treatment and on his recovery went to live at Stocksbridge.[22] Naturally, the story was well-known locally but no-one ever mentioned it to us, no doubt fearing to offend even the most distant relatives.

In 1881 Millhouse was hardly a village. Its cottages were strung out around the former green, in Low Millhouse, or as part of Robin Row, with a few older farm houses nearby. The board school that had been opened in 1879 and the adjoining *Blacksmith's Arms* gave the place some identity where Lee Lane branched off from the main road. The school that I attended from the age of four was the one that my parents had been to. An inscription high on the outside wall told us that it had been erected by the Thurlstone School Board in 1879. Not knowing about local government districts, we were always puzzled why it said Thurlstone when it was in Millhouse; the two

Carlecoates School. Built as a National school in 1836, long before school attendance became compulsory.

J T Smith's grocery and draper's shop, founded in Manchester Road, Thurlstone in 1873.

places were quite distinct to us. The school was built of local stone In the approved neo-Gothic style, resembling a church. It has steeply-sloping slated roofs, large mullioned windows and a bell turret to give it dignity. Iron railings enclosed the yard and the Head Teacher's house stood next door. The school rooms were well lit and open to high ceilings. Further west, another board school was erected at Hazlehead Bar, Carlecoates had its own National School from 1836 and a church from 1857, and Langsett had a combined church and school from 1875.

By 1881 the new village of Millhouse Green had a blacksmith, a joiner, a grocer, and a woman who baked bread for sale, but only two people worked for the local authority. James Wagstaff, a Thurlstone man in origin, was Surveyor to the Local Board. The Head Teacher at the new school was Joseph Ensor, a young married man from Leicester, who lived with his wife and two sons in the master's house next door to the school. John Hinchliffe of Bullhouse Hall, William Smith of Bullhouse Grange and the newly-arrived William Hoyland were the dominant local figures.

Hunshelf and Oxspring Townships

The thin seams of coal and gannister that stretched from Sheffield towards Huddersfield were mined in small pits on the Hunshelf side of the River Don. By 1850 the Henholmes Works of the Armitage company had begun to use the gannister as fireclay and for bricks in reverbatory furnaces. As the population grew in the nineteenth century, the sons of farmers and men with no land to farm turned to mining. Notoriously, children too were forced to earn a living pulling and pushing loaded trucks up the incline to the surface. In his report to the parliamentary commission that inveshtigated child labour in the mines in 1842, the Reverend J C Symons wrote,

> *One of the most disgusting sights I have ever seen was that of young females, dressed like boys in trousers, crawling on all fours, with belts round their waists, and chains passing between their legs, at day pits at Hunshelf bank and in many small pits near Holmfirth and New Mill.*[23]

The horrifying deaths of twenty-six children when Husker pit, near Silkstone, was flooded in 1838 had prompted this investigation, which led to the banning of female and child labour in British mines.

A Sketch of the Life of George Marsh, a Yorkshire Collier (1912)[24] provides vivid personal testimony of the hardship of life that had to be endured by poor children. Born in 1834 at Poole Folds, Hunshelf Bank, he was about four years old when his father died. Late in life, when he was 'one of the oldest and most respected inhabitants of Pilley', Marsh recalled that he was one of eleven children and that, when he was about six years of age, his mother took five of them to the Guardian Room at the *Wortley Arms* (for the Workhouse at Grenoside had not then been built). He lived by begging and at the age of six milked cows at Mr W Newton's Croft Nook Farm in return for his breakfast. A little later he 'drove a mule for him in the day hole [the coal mine] at the back of the new *Rising Sun* at Stocksbridge for five pence a day'. Afterwards he went to work for Mr Willie Jubb, with his brother Jim and Ben Marshall from Bullhouse, 'hurrying in belt and chain from daylight to dark', in other words pulling coal trucks by the method described by Symons. He also worked as a hurrier at other Hunshelf pits and at Hand Bank. To get to work, he 'ran from Poole Folds to there all through the winter, with bare feet and bare legs'. He went barefoot until the age of eleven.

The industrial developments that transformed the peaceful valley of the Little Don on the southern border of Penistone parish and Hunshelf township began slowly in 1794-95 with the erection of a four-storey cotton mill by Jonathan Denton, alongside the old fulling mill. A more significant development was the construction of the Wadsley-Langsett turnpike road along the valley in 1805. Samuel Fox, a Derbyshire man from Bradwell, saw the potential of the site of the (now disused) cotton mill for a wiredrawing business that made huckle and gill-pins for woolcombers. In 1848 he started to make umbrellas with solid steel ribs and three years later one of his employers invented the lightweight, hollow ribs of the Paragon Umbrella. His works also made wire for the crinoline skirts that were fashionable in the late 1850s and 1860s and he began to make his own crucible steel in 1854, but his business was transformed in 1862 when he bought a licence to convert steel by the new Bessemer process. Fox's works now turned to the mass production of rails, billets, springs and rods for the new railways and immigrant workers flocked to the new settlement in the river valley. Stocksbridge became a steel town, which in 1881 had 4,660 inhabitants in 895 houses, a five-fold increase since the mid-nineteenth century. The population rose further to 6,566 in 1901 and 7,090 in 1911. Many of the workers were housed in stone-built terraces, along or to the south of Manchester Road, close to the works, on the opposite side of the river to Hunshelf township, beyond the parish of Penistone. A railway was opened in 1877 to link the steelworks to Deepcar station on the Sheffield-Manchester line.[25]

Another source of employment in Hunshelf township was the large quarry at Green Moor, whose flagstones helped to pave the streets of London and other large cities once the railways provided cheap and efficient transport. The quarry attracted a small settlement, with a school, a Methodist chapel and the *Rock Inn*. Other Hunshelf men and boys found work at the Top and Lower Forges on the opposite bank of the River Don in Wortley township or at the three wireworks in Thurgoland Bottom; some of the Hunshelf militia men had been forgemen or iron rollers in 1806. The Old Mill at Thurgoland, which had been founded as a wireworks in 1624, probably on the site of the Huthwaite fulling mill, was rebuilt in the 1840s and worked until 1926. Downstream, the Tilt Mill and the New Mill also manufactured wire.[26] Dawson's Mill on the Hunshelf-Oxspring township border was also used for wire-drawing by the Camm family in the eighteenth century and John Camm was listed as a wire drawer in the militia returns of 1806. By 1835, however, it had been converted into a woollen mill and by 1852 it was being used for grinding bones as fertiliser. The dam and some low walls survive.[27] The wire trade spread further into Penistone parish once the railways provided cheap transport for raw materials from Sheffield and for finished goods. As we have seen, William Smith moved from Thurgoland to convert the old Millhouse fulling mill into a wireworks, William Hoyland turned the Ecklands Bridge paper mill

Oxspring at the junction of the roads from Thurgoland and Four Lane Ends, with Rolling's steam corn mill on the right.

into an umbrella works, George and John Jagger of the Thurgoland Old Mill altered the mill at Windmill Green into a wire mill and Samuel Fox started off making wire. About 1862 Joseph William Wordsworth of Thurgoland New Mill converted the Oxspring Walk Mill into a wireworks and by 1871 he was employing six men and ten boys. In 1888 George Winterbottom of Dodworth took over the business, making wire for needles and fish hooks.[28]

One more mill needs to be mentioned. The Kirkwood Mill on the western boundary of Oxspring township was fed by a long goit from Castle Dam. It was known as Hawkesworth's scribbling mill at the beginning of the nineteenth century. In 1845 Samuel James Bray of Edale became the manager and converted it into a cloth mill, but from the 1870s it fell into disuse. William Hoyland of Millhouse bought it in 1908, but it was not until 1939 that it was converted into a corn mill by Arnold Goldthorpe, one of the sons of Benjamin Goldthorpe of Bullhouse Mill. The name was changed in 1970 to

Argo Feeds, from the first two letters of Arnold and Goldthorpe, and six years later the successful business of Argo Haulage Penistone Ltd was founded.[29] The employment opportunities at the new mills, including Rolling's steam corn mill, led to the growth of the present village of Oxspring along Sheffield Road and the opening of a board school in 1880. The importance of the various mills in the economy of the Penistone district in the nineteenth and early twentieth centuries is evident. They provided work for large numbers of people and the owners (some of whom, like the Tomassons and the Camms, had shares in other businesses) were able to build substantial stone houses out of their profits and to become the recognised new leaders of local society.

Railways

The opening of the Woodhead Tunnel in 1845 (at the time the longest in Britain at three miles thirteen yards) and the completion of the Lincolnshire-Sheffield-Manchester railway provided opportunities for industrial development and led to great changes in Penistone. A second tunnel was begun in 1847 and opened in 1852. The original workforce of 400 men grew to nearly 1,000 and, at the peak period, to 1,500 as men tunnelled from twelve different rock faces at once. They lived in stone huts at Dunford Bridge and at Woodhead, which was nine miles away from the nearest town, Glossop. Earning good wages and with little else to do, they quickly acquired a reputation for being drunken and dissolute. It was miserable work, for water ran down the sides of the walls and the tunnel was generally ankle-deep and sometimes knee-deep in mud. The job was dangerous too and at least thirty-two men were killed. Another twenty-eight died of cholera at Woodhead in 1849. Serious injuries included 22

Penistone Goods' Yard, Bridge Street. Once the passenger station on the Woodhead line, it was converted to a goods yard when the present station was opened in 1874.

compound fractures, including 2 fractured skulls, 74 simple fractures and another 140 reported cases. In the words of Edwin Chadwick, the public health reformer, the deaths and injuries (more than three per cent killed and fourteen per cent wounded) were 'nearly equal [to] the proportionate casualties of a campaign or a severe battle'. When Wellington Purdon, the assistant engineer at Woodhead, was asked by a House of Commons committee whether the use of a safety fuse would have been beneficial, he gave the notorious reply:

Perhaps it is, but it is attended with such a loss of time, and the difference is so very small, I would not recommend the loss of time for the sake of all the extra lives it would save.[30]

On 1 July 1850 a railway line was opened over a spectacular viaduct of twenty-nine arches from Penistone to Huddersfield, five years after the work was started. Joseph Locke of Barnsley, who had worked on the Sheffield-Manchester line, was the surveyor for a route that needed many tunnels, embankments, cuttings and viaducts along its thirteen miles. These must have seemed a brash addition to the landscape but they have mellowed with time and are now an essential part of the physical character of Penistone parish. The original viaduct at Denby Dale was built of wood in 1846-47 but was partly blown down in a great storm before it was completed; after a fresh start it was opened in 1850. In 1877 Naylor Brothers won a contract to replace it with a graceful, curving, stone viaduct, with twenty-one huge arches, which dominates the village of Denby Dale. This was opened on Whit Sunday, 1880 and the old wooden structure was taken down four years later; its abutment can still be seen on the north-west side of its replacement.[31] Three further mishaps on the local railway lines were captured on film by Joshua Biltcliffe. On 16 July 1884 Bullhouse Bridge was the scene of an horrendous accident on the Sheffield-Manchester line when a locomotive's crank axle broke and the train plunged down the bank, killing 24 people and leaving 64 others seriously injured. On 1 January 1885 4 people died and 40 were injured at an accident at Barnsley Junction and on 2 February 1916

Joshua Biltcliffe was there to record the collapse of the second and third arches of the Penistone to Huddersfield viaduct on 2 February 1916. The line was reopened in August.

the viaduct at the Penistone end of the Huddersfield line collapsed and a locomotive plunged into the valley below.

When another line through Silkstone Common and Dodworth to Barnsley was completed in 1856, Penistone stood at an important junction, linking it with the South Yorkshire coalfield. At first, this new railway line was used only for transporting coal. The present passenger station was opened in 1874, when the original one off St Mary's Street became the goods station. The railways were the prime reason why the founders of the Yorkshire Steel & Iron Works were attracted to Penistone in 1863. They also opened up new markets for local stone, obtained from large quarries at Green Moor and Thurlstone and from smaller ones such as the Rayner family's quarry at Race Common.[32]

Penistone

In his *Tour of the Don* (1837) John Holland noted that

Penistone has often been called in joke 'the finished town' – not from the perfection of its plan, its streets, or its buildings – but from the fact that no additions appear to have been made – no new buildings erected; in short, the laying of one stone upon another in the way of architecture, however humble the erection, is quite a wonder.[33]

This situation was soon to change.

Penistone expanded considerably in the second half of the nineteenth century, after the opening of the Yorkshire Steel & Iron Works to the east of the town. The original proprietors, Benson, Adamson & Garnett, sold their new works the following year to Charles Cammell & Co., the Sheffield steelmaking firm that became Cammell Laird. Each week the new works made 2,000 tons of Bessemer steel ingots, rails, fishplates and axles. At its peak it employed 1,500 men. Old photographs show tall chimneys belching out black smoke beyond the railway station and sidings. The company built seventy houses for its workforce along Sheffield Road in a new settlement that they named Spring Vale, while another group of houses around Don Street were named Spring Gardens, but the new settlement differed from Stocksbridge in that the owners of the steel works did not live nearby. Alternative employment was provided by the flax and thread mills that Messrs Waites erected between Sheffield Road and the River Don about 1860, a short-lived venture that was replaced in 1869 by the Spring Vale Box Works. Further housing for the steelworkers was erected on Castle Green from the 1860s. The closure of Cammell Laird's Penistone works in

Cammell Laird's steelworks in full production in the days when pollution was an accepted consequence of heavy industry.

February 1930, when the firm became part of the English Steel Corporation during the depression following the Wall Street crash, was a devastating blow to the local economy. For five years the site stood unused, but then David Brown Co. took it over to make high-pressure steam turbines and the town's fortunes gradually revived.[34]

The population of Penistone township (which included Spring Vale) increased from 493 in 1801 to 802 in 1851 and then soared to 3,071 in 1901. The 'finished town' acquired a new appearance in Victorian times. The 1854 Ordnance Survey map shows High Street extending southwards towards the new Victoria Street. Soon afterwards, more houses were provided in Ward, Unwin and Clarel Streets and at Penistone Green, which had previously been fields and gardens except for Green House and Joseph Hawley's house, shop, mistals and saw pit. Fearn's Buildings and Garside's Buildings were erected in the Backfields and other late Victorian houses and public buildings were built on the slopes down Church Hill and St Mary's Street and at the crossroads at Bridge End, near the two pubs and Taylor's blacksmith's smithy. The town's streets were named and numbered in November 1881.[35]

The appearance of the town was enhanced by late Victorian buildings such as the Vicarage and the Police Station, the Liberal Club and the Midland Bank, and by private houses such Willow House, the home and surgery of Dr Arthur Wilson, Medical Officer to Penistone and Thurlstone districts. New chapels were erected by the Wesleyans in 1873 and the Methodist New Connection in 1901. After meeting for a while in a cottage in Queen Street, the Spring Vale Primitive Methodists built a 'tin chapel' about 1860, which they replaced in 1927. Penistone Girls' National School was opened in 1823, just below the old grammar school in Kirk Flatt, and soon had 120 pupils. In 1876 St John's National School was opened next door and in 1893 the grammar school moved to a new site at Weirfield, up the hill from the Penistone Poor Law Union Workhouse, which was completed in 1860. The union stretched beyond Penistone parish to include Cawthorne, Clayton West, High Hoyland, Hoylandswaine, Kexbrough, Silkstone and Thurgoland. A Gas Works was opened in 1858 and gas lights were installed in the streets in time for Christmas, 1869. From that year Penistone township was governed by an elected local board, which soon made necessary changes in public health matters. In 1880 Stottercliffe Cemetery replaced the churchyard as the parish burial ground and the Waterworks began to supply piped water from Thurlstone Pumping Station; the Town Pump and public wells such as St Mary's were then closed. The

An aerial view of Penistone in 1966 after the building of new housing estates.

The carters of Cubley Brook Brewery in the days when it was still safe to pose for a photograph in the middle of the road.

construction of reservoirs began at Ingbirchworth in 1868, Midhope in 1897, Langsett in 1904 and Scout Dyke in 1924. A sewage works was ready for use in 1906. Penistone became an Urban District Council in 1894 but the Town Hall was not built until 1914, the year after the Carnegie Fee Library next door.

To the south of the town, Cubley Brook brewery was founded in 1848 by Joseph Brook, maltster and farmer from Kirkburton, who came to live at Old Chapel. The mild and bitter ales that were brewed there supplied the local pubs. Part of the site was converted into a vinegar brewery in 1923.[36] At the top of the hill, near the Victorian Cubley Hall and the weavers' cottages on Joan Royd Lane, Cubley Garden Village or estate was designed by Sir Herbert Baker to house the workforce of Cammell Laird in 1921-22. The gabled cottages that were erected in groups of two or four were built of concrete blocks that were made to look like stone.[37] The Park Avenue housing estate was begun in 1936 and after the war a large council estate was erected at the eastern ends of Unwin, Ward and Victoria Streets. The original Airey houses of the late 1940s, including the one in Unwin Street which we moved to from Catshaw, have been demolished, but the later brick houses are still in use. A generation later, the town expanded to its present size beyond Park Avenue and down the hill towards Water Hall.

Before motor cars transformed communications, the scattered farms and hamlets of the Penistone district remained remote places that were often difficult to get to in winter time. In 1927 Dr Arthur Wilson's reminiscences of fifty years in a moorland practice[38] were of long journeys on horseback or with horse and trap in winters when snow ploughs were not then available. He noted that, 'Penistone is a great place for snow'. He had to charge at the snow drifts in the lanes at a gallop several times until he got through and he recalled that he had been thrown off his horse fourteen times and out of his trap ten times, but never seriously hurt. He told his audience at a meeting of the Yorkshire branch of the British Medical Association that a good deal of a doctor's time in a country practice used to be taken up with midwifery, as very few midwives were available, but he was often called upon to perform surgery:

> *I have amputated two thighs, two arms just below the shoulder, two or three legs, and several forearms.*

He had been forced to operate when it was impossible to get patients

Penistone High Street after the big snow in February 1933.

Penistone celebrates the coronation of King George V in 1911.

into hospital. He recalled that

> *I have removed many breasts and tumours, and operated upon several empyemas with removal of a piece of rib. I have operated also for fistula and for strangulated hernia. The operations were nearly all done on the bed, as at small cottages there was no room to improvise an operation table.*

He remembered epidemics of influenza, smallpox, typhoid fever, scarlet fever and diphtheria and, particularly, the international influenza epidemic of October and November 1918, at the close of the First World War, when in seventeen days he visited 833 houses and saw 1,219 patients.

Chapter Nine

Catshaw in the 1940s

✠

The old farmhouse at Catshaw has been extended and modernised to make it a suitable place for present-day living. It is now a far better dwelling than it was when we lived there in the 1940s. But the shell of the old house is still plain to see. We were tenants (at a rent of three shillings a week) of the central part, between the barn and the nineteenth century addition to the house. The cottage that we occupied was the old stone farmhouse that had been built in the eighteenth century. My childhood friend, Roger Goldthorpe, has returned to the home of his ancestors and has made it more commodious by extending it at the rear and adding a porch over the front door. His sister, Mavis, who took me to school in my earliest years, lives next door, where my mother's sister and her family lived when I was a boy. Several other members of the family live nearby. The Goldthorpes have lived in the hamlet for nearly two hundred years, but now they occupy it as never before.

The old farmhouse was built of the local millstone grit and given a stone slate roof in the traditional manner. The ivy which covered much of our front wall has been stripped away, revealing the straight

The old farmhouse at Catshaw in the late 1930s, with the author's mother and grandmother.

The author, aged 4, at Catshaw in 1943.

joint between the old house and the nineteenth-century extension. The newer part was empty when I was born, but a year later my mother's younger sister and her family moved in. Their house consisted of a large downstairs room and kitchen and two bedrooms. On the other side of our part of the old farmhouse a barn had been constructed along the same roof line in the typical Pennine manner. Historians call these buildings 'laithe houses', from the old northern dialect word for a barn. It is a useful term for a type of building that is characteristic of the Yorkshire and Lancashire Pennines but which is rarely found in the Derbyshire part of the Peak District, just a few miles further south. Unlike the 'long houses' of some other parts of England, the house and barn were not connected internally. A huge, arched doorway allowed the passage of loaded hay carts into the barn. Some of the cows were housed in a mistal at the far end of the barn and on still nights we could hear them from inside the house. I did not realise that mistal was a local dialect term until I went to university and no-one knew what I was talking about.

The stone-flagged path that led from our door along the farmyard wall to a gate in the wall by the lane was built in 1939, at the same time as improvements were being made to the house next door before my aunty and uncle moved in. A parallel path and wall enclosed our joint garden to the east. The land in front of the two properties was not divided, nor was it cultivated or kept in trim, but until she moved away in 1943 my grandmother kept a few hens here in small hen-cotes and runs marked out by stakes and chicken wire. A large sycamore tree that reared up in the lane immediately beyond our wall was used by the Home Guard during the Second World War for their exercises. Men hid in the branches and fired blank ammunition at attackers who crept along the field walls from Bullhouse Mill and round the back of the cottages at the other side of the lane. The same manoeuvre was repeated every few weeks. It was real 'Dad's Army' stuff. I rushed out to collect the blank cartridges as soon as the soldiers were gone. Fields came right up to the rear of our house and to the side of my aunty and uncle's. A large manure stack behind the barn had such a powerful odour and attracted so many flies in summer time that the small window in our rear kitchen had to be kept closed most of the time.

It is worth describing our house in detail because it was entirely typical of the local rural dwellings of the time. The door to the house had no lock, only a latch, or sneck as we called it, but it could be fastened from the inside by a wooden bar. The Yorkshire expression to close the door was 'to put t'wood in t'oil (the hole)' and a derogatory exclamation against someone who couldn't throw straight was 'Tha couldn't hit a barn door if tha were sat on t'sneck'. The door led into a large ground-floor room that we called 'the house'. This terminology sounds confusing to outsiders but it was commonly used in Pennine districts and dates back to the time when houses were simple one-roomed buildings open to the rafters. Many of our dialect words were archaic expressions that had died out in other parts of the country. A lean-to at the rear of the house contained an unheated kitchen and a pantry.

A sash window with a sill eighteen inches wide lit this ground-floor room. The original window has been widened slightly because of modern light regulations, but it could not be extended far because of the lintel stone above it. Its present proportions are not very different from before, but it has been double-glazed and is not in the drab, unpainted condition that I was familiar with. A couch was placed below the window and a piece of furniture that we optimistically called a wardrobe stood between the window and the door. A little stool that was bought for my father when he was a child and which I still possess was placed between the couch and the fireplace.

On entering our door, the fireplace caught the eye. Set in the middle of the wall that separated us from my Aunty Rosy's, it formed part of a 'Yorkshire range' cast in iron and kept clean and bright by the arduous process of 'black leading'. Every morning the ashes had to be shovelled out of the grate and a fire of newspaper, sticks and coal set alight. Often it was necessary to place a sheet of newspaper against the chimney breast to draw the fire. We soon learned the art of removing the paper when it started to turn brown by singeing, otherwise the burning paper would shoot up the chimney with the risk of the soot catching fire. Sending for a chimney sweep was an expense that was put off as long as possible. One of my jobs as I got older was to chop the firewood from old pit props that my father brought home. As a miner, he also received free loads of coal from time to time. These were brought by lorry and tipped in the lane, so it was a strenuous job getting the coal inside. I cannot remember where we stored it, but perhaps we used the cellar. A bucket full of coal always stood ready by the fireplace.

A square boiler that held over two gallons of water stood to the left of the fireplace. High bars from which vessels could be hung stretched across the fire. To the right was an oven, heated by the fire. Above it, on a shelf known as 'top of t'oven', the pots and pans were kept. Two feet above this shelf a mantelpiece framed the whole range. A clock occupied the central place on the mantelpiece, with a tea caddy, match boxes, candlesticks, letters and cards, and other odds and ends surrounding it. Two china cats stood at the ends and a mirror was hung above. All our cooking was done on the fire or in the oven. We had no

Part of the Biltcliffe tradition. A photograph of my mother, myself, my sister Barbara and my borther Ernest, taken in J T Biltcliffe's studio in the late 1940s.

supply of hot water, so everything had to be heated on the fire in pans.

A set pot was fixed in the corner to the right of the oven, its brick frame supporting a bowl-shaped, metal 'pot'. I suppose that these pots really were earthenware when they were first made. Later on, when I took local history classes, I could always provoke a fierce discussion by asking what the difference was between a set pot and a copper. We usually came to the conclusion that we were talking about the same thing. A fire was lit under the set pot to heat water on wash days, which of course were every Monday. A round lid for the pot kept the water hot. Water was topped up from the boiler by means of an enamel ladling can, which could hold six pints, and the same can was used to take hot water to the washer in the kitchen. This washer had been an expensive item, costing over £8, when my parents had married. It was worked by the constant pulling of a handle and was considered better than the usual posser. On wet or cold days the washing was hung to dry on a wooden frame over the fire and all the windows got steamed up. The smoothing iron had to be heated on the fire before it could be used.

The other weekly event was Friday night bath time. The tin bath was brought out of the kitchen and set in front of the fire, where pans of hot water were kept on the boil. We children took it in turns, starting with the youngest. Fresh hot water was added from time to time. Grandad sat in one of the two wooden, high-backed chairs that were placed on each side of the fireplace, towel in hand, ready to dry our hair by a brisk rubbing which made our scalps tingle. A wire fireguard enclosed the fireplace completely when we were young. The bath was placed on the stone flags of the floor, so that it didn't matter too much if we splashed the water, but we stepped out on to the pegged rug in front of the fire. These rugs are now rarely seen outside museums but they were once found in nearly every home in the neighbourhood. Their manufacture was a family enterprise around the fire in the winter months. The base was a piece of sacking which determined the size and shape of the finished rug. Old clothes were cut up into short, rectangular ribbons, two holes were pierced in the sacking by the point of a pear-shaped wooden peg, then the peg was used again to push the ribbon through the holes. The art was in the making of coloured patterns in the finished article. Pegged rugs looked and felt wonderful for a few days, or even weeks, but they soon wore flat and lost their cheerful colour. They were warm, cheap and serviceable but difficult to keep clean. In the days before vacuum cleaners, they were shaken outside the house and beaten against a wall.

The ceiling was a low one and its beams needed constant cleaning, for they attracted smoke from the fire and soot from the paraffin lamp. The beams have now been covered with plaster board, but originally they could be seen to support the bedroom floorboards, which painted white. The staircase was placed immediately behind the door, by the wall that divided the house from the barn. The cupboard under the stairs acted as a 'cubby-hole' for odds-and-ends. Beyond it, and obscured by a set of drawers, a door led into the kitchen. The remaining wall acted as the backcloth for a mahogany set of drawers and a piano. Another pegged rug covered most of the space in front of the the piano and the two sets of drawers. Elsewhere, the stone flags were covered with a large piece of coconut matting. One of our two best mahogany chairs was placed by the piano and the other stood in the corner to the left of the kitchen door. Two more chairs fitted under the sturdy square table that stood in the centre of the house. We spent much of our time sitting around it, eating our meals or playing games, such as draughts, cards, ludo and the joining of dots by lines into 'boxes'. A paraffin lamp was

Bullhouse Chapel Sunday School children at an anniversary concert in March 1949. Spot the author!

supported from a hook in one of the ceiling beams above. It all sounds rather cluttered and I suppose it was by modern standards of comfort, but the room was a large one which was snug and warm when the fire was blazing and cheerful when the mantle of the lamp was new and bright. But most evenings the room was dark, with flickering shadows. The mantle required constant attention to keep a steady glow and to stop it bursting into flames and black smoke.

The kitchen was not at all like the kitchens of today, for the cooking was not done there. It consisted of a one-storey lean-to with no fire, but with the convenience of running water from a tap above the stone sink. This was where we washed ourselves in the morning and cleaned our teeth. A little table stood by the sink and here were kept the washer, the mangle, the brush and the ladling can. Food was kept on stone shelves in a pantry and the vegetables were scraped and cut at the sink. Light came from the little square panes of the rear window. I expect the lean-to was part of the original building, for I have found plenty of historical evidence of unheated kitchens in Pennine farm houses, but I do not mourn its demolition to make way for the modern extension. It was a cold, cheerless place in winter time.

We needed a candle to light ourselves to bed. Climbing the stairs could be rather difficult, for in winter time we also carried something to keep us warm. We had no hot water bottles, so we had to improvise. My wife and children think I am pulling their legs when I tell them that I had a brick that had been heated in the oven and wrapped in a blanket. If we forgot to put the brick in the oven the oven shelf was used instead. This method of warming the bed was an inefficient one, for one part of the bed was very hot and the rest was cold, and I had to be careful to keep the blanket wrapped around the brick or shelf so that I didn't get burnt.

The upper floor had originally been one big bedroom, but it had long since been partitioned into two, each with its sash window. A cot occupied the space in the gap between the stairs and the door into our parents' bedroom. Their furniture consisted of a bed in the corner by the partition, a blanket box under the window, and a chest of drawers, a wash stand and a wardrobe. Another door led into the children's bedroom. I had the small bed in the corner by the window which looked out over the path to the garden gate, with a clear view of the farmyard to the right. My sister, Barbara, my brother, Ernest, and my cousin, Lena, shared the large bed. The floor was covered with linoleum and the walls were papered with a paste made of flour and water. It was often so cold in winter time that the window panes were covered with delicate frost patterns. We daren't complain in case we were considered 'nesh'. Under our beds we had chamber pots, or 'poes' as they were called in Yorkshire (I have never seen the word spelt!), a necessary convenience at night time when the alternative was a to run across the farmyard to the earth lavatory behind the barn. This was a smelly place that attracted flies in summer until the council men came in their lorry to empty it. A wooden seat had two holes in it, the smallest for the children. Sheets of newspaper had to suffice as our toilet paper.

The house also had an attic and a cellar, but we children kept clear of them. The attic was approached through a door on the landing and Grandma Hey, who lived with us until my brother was born, had kept a few old hen things in it. Now the space has been converted into a bathroom. We feared the possibility of rats in the cellar but they probably existed only in our imagination; we certainly never saw one. Field mice, on the other hand, were ever present in old farmhouses and cottages. In the stillness of the night we sometimes saw one glide silently across the fireplace. Mother regarded them as a personal affront and was triumphant when she trapped one, but we children were amused by them. We had a very different attitude to the large beetles, which we called blackclocks. They liked the heat of the fire and were a persistent nuisance in all old houses, in the towns as well as the countryside. They only came out when it was dark and we could never get rid of them. Our other enemy was the common house fly in summer time. We had no sprays to kill them and had to rely on the primitive method of hanging sticky paper from the ceiling in the hope that they would get caught. These strips of gluey paper were bought at shops, so they must have been in common use. Surprisingly, they did catch a large number of flies, but they were very irritating when you walked into them!

A gate led into the farmyard immediately to the right of our door. A water trough for the animals stood at the other side of our wall. Cats roamed about the farm buildings and when a large litter of kittens were born, we watched in fascinated horror as Billy Goldthorpe, the farmer, picked them up in turn and drowned all but one in the trough. The cat seemed contended enough to be left with just the one. Cats helped to keep the mice down but they would have been a nuisance themselves if they had been allowed to multiply. A mistal for a dozen cows and a stable for the horse stood across the farmyard by the lane. We watched Billy milk his dairy shorthorns and were occasionally allowed to try ourselves. After milking, Billy went round to each house with his pail, but most of his milk was poured into metal churns to await collection on a lorry. Barns formed two sides of the farmyard, one in line with our house and the other at right angles to it. This other barn was framed with sturdy timbers and I have always regretted that they were removed (with considerable difficulty) before I had sufficient expertise to date them. I suspect that they were part of the oldest building at Catshaw.

Early in the Second World War, the government decided to survey all the farms in the country, so that they would have a clear picture of what food was being produced. On 24 January 1942 the surveyors came to Catshaw and recorded the crops and livestock of Mr W O Goldthorpe of Moorland View, the owner of the 35½ acres of Catshaw Farm:[1]

A present-day view of Catshaw from Bullhouse.

The workforce at Bullhouse Mill, including my Uncle Arthur and members of the Goldthorpe family, prepare to join the procession to Penistone to celebrate the coronation of King George V in 1911.

6¹/₂ acres oats, ³/₄ acre potatoes, ³/₄ acre turnips and swedes, 2 acres kale (for fodder).
11 acres permanent grass for mowing, 15 acres permanent grass for grazing.
3 cows and a heifer in milk, 1 heifer in calf, six female calves 1 to 2 years old, 5 bull calves.
90 fowls, six months or more old, 60 fowls under six months.
2 mares.

Farmers were classified A, B or C according to their competence. Billy Goldthorpe was in the top class, as indeed were most of the other local farmers. They were doing the best they could with the land and technology at their disposal. Moorland View was the name of the house that the Goldthorpes had built across the lane from the original farmhouse, where we lived. It was the only modern house in Catshaw, but it did not then have its present cladding of stone.

The housing conditions at Catshaw in the 1940s seem unbelievable to people who were born a generation or two later and to those who were brought up in towns, but our life-style was in no way unusual in the countryside around Penistone at that time. Almost everyone we knew lived in similar circumstances and at the same standard of living. The better equipped houses had electric lights, flush toilets and bathrooms. Our way of life had more in common with the eighteenth and nineteenth centuries than with the present day. We had no difficulty in understanding how our ancestors had lived.

Coal Mining

My father left Millhouse School at the age of twelve in 1916, the year that his father died. He began work as a bricklayer but the post-war slump affected that trade badly. The miners' strike in 1921 had just ended, so at the age of seventeen he went to work down the pit. He was working at Bullhouse Colliery in May 1926 when the General Strike began. For most workers it was over in days, but the miners held out until November, when the onset of winter forced them back underground. The General Strike was the formative event in my father's working life. The bitterness of the defeat was a sour memory that never went away. By the late 1930s he had fallen out with the managers at Bullhouse and was working at Stocksbridge, even though this involved a bus journey rather than a short walk across the fields. A shaft in the middle of Samuel Fox's steelworks was used until a new shaft was sunk in Sheephouse Wood. It took about forty minutes to walk underground to the coal face, but miners were paid from the time that they clocked in at the surface. Stocksbridge pit closed in 1943, but my father did not go back to Bullhouse. Instead, he found a job at the Hepworth Iron Company's Sledbrook Colliery at Crowedge, a couple of miles beyond Catshaw. He worked there until he fell ill in 1957. He had been a miner for thirty-six years. The pits at Crowedge and Bullhouse both closed in the early 1960s, their seams exhausted long before those of the larger pits further east.

The miners at Sledbrook Colliery had to walk only a quarter-of-a-mile or so down the inclined shaft, a journey that took them about fifteen minutes. The pits in this district were very different from the deep mines at the heart of the South Yorkshire Coalfield, where the colliers descended in cages to work the six-foot Barnsley seam. The miners at Sledbrook worked a twenty-two-inch coal seam and the associated bed of gannister, which was hard and had to be left to weather before it could be used as fireclay. My birth certificate describes my father as a coal hewer, someone who used a pick and a shovel to hack the coal from the face. When he was older, his job was to shovel the coal on to the conveyor belt.

Three shifts were worked at Sledbrook. The morning one lasted from 6.00 am to 2.00 pm, the afternoon from 2.00 pm to 10.00 pm, and the night shift from 10.00 pm to 5.30 am. When he lived at Catshaw, my father worked the daytime shifts, but in later life he worked at night, preparing work for the men who came in the morning. About forty miners were employed at Sledbrook, but only five or six of these worked the night shift. The colliery had a rope haulage system to move the loaded waggons; no pit ponies were used.

My father (fourth from the left on the back row) and other Millhouse and Thurlstone men on a day out at Blackpool.

A fan sent fresh air down a ventilation shaft, so that the temperature at the coal face was the same as on the surface. In the deeper, hotter pits men wore only their drawers, but Dad worked in a vest and trousers, held up by a thick belt. Pads were strapped round his knees and clogs were deemed more serviceable than boots. He took cold, milk-less tea in a Tizer bottle to drink while he ate the sandwiches that my mother had packed in his snap tin. His helmet and lamp were kept at the 'clocking-in' room at the pit head; in his early days he had used a hand-held lamp. The thin seam that was worked at Stocksbridge, Bullhouse and Sledbrook did not leak gas that might explode, but the colliers were constantly aware of the danger of roof falls and the risk of injury from machinery. Dad's back was once hurt in a roof fall and another man at Sledbrook died after being electrocuted. The greatest threat was a long-term, hidden one – the onset of pneumoconiosis from inhaling the dust generated by shot firing. We were not aware of this danger as children, but we saw how my Dad's knees would sometimes swell alarmingly and painfully. The colliers and the doctors both referred to this condition as beat knees, brought on by the strain of working while bent double and by kneeling in cold water. He once gave us a scare by getting gangrene.

To get to work, my father caught a Baddeley's bus at Catshaw

Cross. The miners did not have special buses then. I well remember the groans of those of us who were travelling by bus to Barnsley in the 1950s whenever we caught sight of a queue of blackened miners waiting to join us at Dodworth at the end of their shift. Genial though they were, and amused as we all pretended to be, care was taken not to get our clothes soiled by contact with their grime. The miners had to wash at home, starting with their top half in the sink then soaking themselves in a tin bath in front of the fire.

Wage levels in the pits were comparable with those in the steelworks, but with a young family to rear a miner had to keep in work. The National Health Service, brought in by the Labour Government after the war, made a huge difference, but my father continued to belong to a friendly society that provided insurance in times of ill health. It always amused us that a coal miner belonged to The Ancient Order of Loyal Shepherds, but the benefits were real. I was sometimes trusted to walk to Thurlstone with the subscription. In the 1930s, in the aftermath of the General Strike, the local pits did not allow trade unions. Many of the miners were also small farmers, so they did not feel the need to band together to bargain their wage rates. After the nationalisation of coal mining in 1947, however, small pits such as these were licensed to continue operating provided they paid their workforce the nationally-agreed rates. John Moore, a foreman at Sledbrook Colliery and a Methodist lay preacher, told me about the acrimonious arguments with the managers, who often did not pay all the claims.

1947

By general agreement, the winters of 1933, 1947 and 1962-63 are reckoned to have been the worst in the twentieth century. The people of the Penistone district are in absolutely no doubt that the winter of 1947 was the hardest to endure. Snow fell to a greater depth in 1933, but it did not last long; the winter of 1962-63 was bad enough, but technology had advanced and so we managed better; the winter of 1947 came in the years of austerity after a long war and in the midst of a fuel crisis, and it lasted much longer than the others. It was bitterly cold for weeks.

The *Penistone Almanack*[2] for 1948 ran a special feature on the weather of the previous year. 'We shall remember the discomfort and dislocation between January 24th and March 16th', it began, 'caused by a winter unequalled in severity since 1814, which affected four-fifths of Great Britain'. At first, the snow was unexceptional for the time of year, but the front page of the *Barnsley Chronicle*[3] on

Saturday, 8 February reported and illustrated 'picturesque scenes after the greatest blizzard for years'. This had begun the previous weekend and had continued through the week, so that,

> *many people had to dig themselves out of their houses through drifts*
> *four feet deep... In the Penistone area a high wind drifted the snow in*
> *many places to a depth of six to eight feet.*

The 'Langsett circular' and other buses had to be cancelled and workers were unable to get to Samuel Fox's or David Brown's. Several collieries ceased working because the deep snow prevented miners from reaching them. Even before the snow, coal stocks were becoming exhausted. Electricity cuts were ordered to save fuel. The newspaper reported that,

> *As many people were without fuel there is a daily trek to the Penistone*
> *Gas Works of people with sledges, barrows and all kinds of transport to*
> *obtain coke. Many householders are faced with a shortage of bread*
> *and have had to bake their own.*

Schools and churches closed through lack of heating.

The *Penistone Almanack* noted how transport services were reduced to impotency. All bus services were stopped completely for two days and again on 25 February. Huddersfield buses to Penistone were turned back at Shepley, those from Barnsley got no further than Silkstone, and the Baddeley bus service over the hills from Holmfirth to Penistone was suspended for six weeks. Catshaw was cut off completely, but life was even harder further west. The *Almanack* remembered that, 'Crowedge, Carlecoates and Dunford suffered badly, having neither rail nor road transport'. The Woodhead Tunnel was blocked and two hundred Poles, who had remained after the war because of the Russian occupation of their country, were called in to clear the snow. The tunnel was blocked repeatedly and all trains terminated at Sheffield. 'Crowedge, which depends on paraffin for lighting, which was difficult to obtain, had worse to bear'. Hazlehead had no postal deliveries for over a week and telephone wires and poles were brought down by the weight of the snow. Drifts piled up until they were fourteen feet high, and 'one man walking on the highroad at Ewden found that he had walked over an embedded car'. Farmers lost hundreds of sheep on the moors. For a time, milk could not be collected at farms, nor could coal and coke be delivered. A 'constant stream of sledges' went to and from the Penistone Goods Station for coal and the Gas Works for coke; up to fifty sledges at a time could be seen waiting for supplies.

The Square Cottage at Hartcliff, where my mother lived as a girl from 1919 to 1920. It occupied the rough piece of land at the junction of the roads from Penistone and Brockholes. Part of the walls were still standing in the 1960s, but the site has since been cleared.

The intensity of the cold and the length of the winter are remembered as much as the size of the snow drifts. Huge icicles hung from houses and barns and sparkled in the bright blue skies. Other days were grey and dreary, when ice hung heavily on wires and trees. Reports filtered through of heroic journeys made by doctors and of the difficulties faced by funeral parties making their way from Dunford through six miles of snow to Stottercliffe Cemetery. When seventy-four-year old George Fox died at Royd Farm, Millhouse, his coffin had to be taken to the cemetery by sledge over the snow.

At Catshaw we were surrounded by drifts until the men dug a passage through the snow across the field to Lee Lane. It seemed an heroic achievement. We had not been able to get to school for a fortnight. We walked along the tops of walls, which we could just see through the snow. The electricity cuts did not affect us for we had no supply at the best of times, but the lack of a proper toilet was mourned as we trudged across the icy farmyard. More alarming was the shortage of coal, the source of all our heat. Desperate remedies were called for and one dark night I walked with Dad across the fields to Hazlehead Hall, then down the track that led us across the Don and up to the railway embankment. There we picked pieces of coal that had fallen off the loaded train waggons and put them in a sack to carry home. When a train came past, we lay flat against the ground so that we could not be seen. I was only eight years old at the time but I can remember thinking how absurd it was that we were short of coal and had to resort to such indignities when my father spent his working life digging it out.

The winter ended with widespread flooding as the snow thawed rapidly and with the wettest March for ninety years. Double Summer Time was introduced on 13 April in order to save light and fuel. The weather then turned exceptionally warm. On the evening of 10 May an electric storm with forked lightning and thunder brought torrential rain. A similar storm on 29 May ended the hottest day in May for sixty-five years. June was scorchingly hot. On 2 June the hottest June day for sixty-two years was followed by the hottest June night ever recorded. Records continued to be broken. From 5 August to 5 September no rain fell in the Penistone district. We watched with growing concern while the heather and bilberry bushes below Hartcliff Summer House were consumed with fire. Shortage of water meant that the Fire Brigade could do little but try to contain the fire. It blazed for ten days and came perilously close to Hartcliff Hall. Those who still depended on well water found that their supplies dried up. Some farmers in the Hoylandswaine area had to carry water nearly a mile. On the brighter side, the harvest was the earliest and easiest for over a generation. But in that year Billy Goldthorpe's mare, Lady, died and the horse-drawn era gave way to that of the tractor.

Billy Goldthorpe's mother was Martha Hey, my grandfather's younger sister. His wife, Sarah Green, was the sister of my Uncle Percy, who lived next door to us. We seemed to have family connections all around. The nearness of the homes of our relations seems unusual now but was perfectly normal in the 1940s. My mother's parents lived in a cottage across the lane at Catshaw, my father's mother lived with his sister and her son only

Hartcliff Summer House (now demolished), which was built by Henry Richardson in 1856, the same year that he erected Hartcliff Tower.

Millhouse Green, seen from Hartcliff, before the expansion of the village.

a field or two away at Mirefield and nearly all my numerous cousins lived within walking distance at Millhouse and Thurlstone or on nearby farms. We took a short bus ride only when we visited my mother's elder sister and her family at Stocksbridge. This ancient pattern began to change in the 1950s, when several of my cousins emigrated to Australia, but I still have numerous relations in the Penistone district. Many another local family can tell a similar story. Family history and local history were two sides of the same coin.

Old photographs from the 1940s reveal a world that was normal and acceptable to us, for we knew no other, but one that now seems incredibly old-fashioned. When I became an historian and started to study rural societies in the seventeenth and eighteenth centuries I found a way of life that was familiar to me – a world of horses and carts, hay cocks and corn stacks, manure heaps and privvy middens, corn mills and small collieries, and farmhouses where the cooking was done on the open fire. I found it easy to empathise.

Notes

Chapter 1
1 A H Smith, *The Place-Names of the West Riding of Yorkshire, I* (Cambridge, English Place-Name Society, 1961), p.339.
2 Sheffield Archives, Crewe, 705.
3 Revd J Hunter, *Familiae Minorum Gentium*, 5 vols (Harleian Society, 1895), pp.40-41.
4 Borthwick Institute of Historical Research, York: Doncaster deanery wills and inventories; Sheffield Archives, Crewe, 933.
5 Thomas Jeffreys's map was reprinted by Harry Margary of Lympne Castle, Kent, in 1973 and is available at local record offices or the local studies departments of major public libraries.
6 'Yorkshire Diaries and Autobiographies in the Seventeenth and Eighteenth Centuries', *Surtees Society*, LXV (1875), p.59.

Chapter 2
1 Revd J Hunter, *South Yorkshire: the History and Topography of the Deanery of Doncaster, II* (London, 1831), p. 221.
2 The acreages are the ones quoted in W Page, ed., *The Victoria History of the County of York*, III (London, 1913), p. 542. Earlier figures, quoted in the official publication, *Census of Great Britain, 1851: Population Tables*, II (London, 1852), underestimated the moorland acreages before the Ordnance Survey made an accurate survey.
3 A H Thompson and C Clay, eds, 'Fasti Parochiales', II *Yorkshire Archaeological Society Record Series*, CVII, (1943), pp. 18-26.
4 The hospital was rebuilt in 1827 in Shrewsbury Road by Norfolk Park, Sheffield, where it still provides accommodation for senior citizens.
5 'Register of Archbishop Walter de Gray, 1215-65', *Surtees Society*, LVI (1872).
6 Borthwick Institute of Historical Research, York: archbishop's registers, 1479 and 1495 (Silkstone) and 1486 indulgence (Almondbury); the will of John Skires, 1497, contains a bequest towards completing Wentworth church tower.
7 J W Clay, ed., 'Yorkshire Church Notes, 1619-31, by Roger Dodsworth', *Yorkshire Archaeological Society Record Series*, XXXIV, (1904), pp. 1-2.
8 Hunter, II, pp. 341-42.
9 See note 7.
10 Borthwick Institute of Historical Research, York, R.1.29.97, Holgate's Register.
11 As in most churchyards, the earliest tombstones at Penistone date from the late seventeenth century. Occasionally, a tombstone records an earlier event, but it is clear from the lettering that this records the death of an ancestor and is not contemporary with that death. The absence of early tombstones throws even more doubt on the unlikely (but widely-believed) story that the blind Dr Nicholas Saunderson learned to read by tracing the letters on the tombstones in the churchyard.
12 J N Dransfield, *History of Penistone* (Penistone, 1906), pp. 163-64.
13 Hunter, II, pp. 334, 342. The chapel is mentioned in 1452 in J W Walker, ed., 'Abstracts of the Chartularies of the Priory of Monkbretton', *Yorkshire Archaeological Society Record Series*, LXVI (1924), p. 145, when it was said to stand alongside 'a messuage or plot of land called Coblay'. The original Cubley was therefore by Cubley Brook; by 1475 it belonged to Monk Bretton Priory.
14 Sheffield Archives, Crewe, 1092.
15 Hunter, II, p. 342.
16 Revd J Hunter, ed., *Letters of Eminent Men Addressed to Ralph Thoresby, FRS* (London, 1832).
17 Sheffield Archives, Wilson deeds, 424. Could the John del Rodes who was instrumental in founding the grammar school in 1392 be the custodian of St John's chapel?

Chapter 3
1 Revd J Hunter, *South Yorkshire: the History and Topography of the Deanery of Doncaster*, II (London, 1831), pp. 333-34. Joan, another daughter of John de Peniston, also granted property within the manor to William Clarel in 1297.
2 Sheffield Archives, Crewe, 626, 631, 720, 833, 925, 1003 and 1054.
3 Nottinghamshire Archives, DD SR 26/2; Sheffield Archives, SYCRO, 560/F/3/2.
4 Catalogue of Ancient Deeds in the Public Record Office, I, c. 310: Elizabeth, late wife of Nicholas de Wordesworth of Penistone, was granted a tenement in Thurlstone township called Copstorth, which seems to be the place known later as Copster. The Wordsworths owned this mill in the sixteenth and seventeenth centuries; V Nicholson, *Upper Don Watermills* (Sheffield, 2001), pp. 109-16.
5 The manor was divided between two heiresses of the Foljambes, whose rights passed to the Wordsworths and the Copleys of Nether Hall, Doncaster. The Copleys sold their part to the Wordsworths in 1750.
6 e.g. 1645 grant to Ambrose Wadsworth of Schole Hill, yeoman (Sheffield Archives, SYC Archives, 560/F/8/1); in his will of 1663 Ralph Wordsworth of Water Hall referred to all his children as Wadsworth (Borthwick Institute of Historical Research, York: Doncaster deanery wills). See G Redmonds, *Surnames and Genealogy: a new approach* (Boston, New England, 1997) about the ways in which surnames could change.
7 J W Walker, 'Abstracts of the Chartularies of the Priory of Monkbretton', *Yorkshire Archaeological Society Record Series*, LXVI (1924), p. 145; Sheffield Archives, Crewe, 621. E Ekwall, *The Oxford Dictionary of English Place-Names* (Oxford, 1951), p.474 gives 'Wordelword' as a spelling of Wardleworth about 1200.
8 *The Returns of the Poll Tax for the West Riding of Yorkshire, 1379* (Yorkshire Archaeological and Topographical Association, 1882). William Waterhall, the son and heir of Richard Waterhall, is recorded in J W Walker, p. 145. Intriguingly, William de Peniston held land in Tottington, close to Turton, in 1212 and his descendants still owned this property in 1292; see W Farrer and J Brownbill, eds, *The Victoria History of the County of Lancaster*, V (1911), p. 145, note.

9 Sheffield Archives, SYC Archives, 560/F/3/3.
10 'A Selection of Wills from the Registry at York', *Surtees Society*, 53 (1869), p. 147.
11 W E Spencer, 'The Wordsworth Family', in J Addy, ed., *A Further History of Penistone* (Penistone, 1965), pp. 64-74, supplemented by information from Sheffield Archives, Crewe muniments. It is intriguing that Josias Wordsworth chose to purchase and rebuild Wadworth Hall, near Doncaster, but the family name was never written as Wadworth.
12 Sheffield Archives, Crewe, 1092.
13 East Yorkshire Record Office, Beverley, DDBM/7-9.
14 Smith, I, pp. 337-8; Scholes derives from a Viking word for a temporary summer pasture, but it acquired other meanings, such as labourers' cottages and the place where cows that grazed on the commons were milked. 'The commonfield of Scoles' is recorded in 1441 in Sheffield Archives, Crewe, 621.
15 C E Whiting, ed., 'Two Yorkshire Diaries', *Yorkshire Archaeological Society Record Series*, CXVII (1952), p. 17 mentions Penistone races in 1732.
16 Hunter, II, pp. 354-56.
17 Hunter, II, p. 347.
18 P F Ryder, 'Oxspring Lodge', *Post-Medieval Archaeology*, 19 (1985), pp. 49-62.
19 Hunter, II, p. 354; J Holland, *Tour of the Don*, (Sheffield, 1837), p. 78; Nicholson, pp. 151-63.
20 Hunter, II, p. 355; Smith, I, 335.
21 Sheffield Archives, Crewe, 1743; D Hey, ed., *The Militia Men of the Barnsley District, 1806: an analysis of the Staincross militia returns* (Sheffield, 1998; available on microfiche from the Sheffield and District Family History Society).
22 Nicholson, p. 144.
23 T W Hall, *A Descriptive Catalogue of the Bosville and Lindsay Collections* (Sheffield, 1930), p. 28; Sheffield Archives, ACM S116; Catalogue of the Talbot Correspondence, 2/71.
24 Hall, *Bosville and Lindsay*, pp. 16-18.
25 East Yorkshire Record Office, DDBM/17/1.
26 Barnsley Archives, enclosure awards.
27 Sheffield Archives, Wharncliffe muniments, 32.
28 Nicholson, pp 145-50.
29 Nicholson, pp. 131-38.
30 M Gelling and A Cole, *The Landscape of Place-Names* (Stamford, 2000), pp. 216-19.
31 P Crossland, 'Hunshelf Hall' in W. G. Hoskins, ed., *History from the Farm* (London, 1970), pp. 91-94; Hunter, II, p. 356.
32 Gelling and Cole, p. 571. The place-name element -carr is derived from Old Norse *kjarr*. Hunter, II, p. 356; J. Kenworthy, *Annals and Antiquities of the Little Don and Ewden Valley* (Deepcar, 1914), pp. 9-28; J. Branston, *Stocksbridge and Neighbourhood* (Stocksbridge, no date), p. 39.
33 J Kenworthy, *Town Fields and Commons of Hunshelf, Langsett and Waldershelf* (Deepcar, 1917).
34 Smith, I, p. 329; T W Hall, *A Descriptive Catalogue of the Wheat Collection* (Sheffield, 1920), p.2. Matthew de Snodenhill witnessed a deed about 1300 (Sheffield Archives, SYC Archives, 560F/3/3).
35 Smith, I, pp. 332, 336-37.
36 M Gelling, *Place-Names in the Landscape* (London, 1984), pp. 100-11, 182-83.
37 J N Dransfield, *History of Penistone* (1906), p. 267.
38 Leeds University, Brotherton Library, Wilson collection, CLIX, 96.
39 Sheffield Archives, Spencer-Stanhope, 1154.
40 Bradford, West Yorkshire Archive Service, Spencer-Stanhope, 1054; *Calendar of Charter Rolls*, I (Record Commissioners, 1837), p. 383.
41 *List and Index Society, Supplementary Series*, III, vol. 2 (1964), p. 261.
42 Calendar of Charter Rolls, II, p.353, III, p. 107. See also W Farrer, ed., *Early Yorkshire Charters*, III (1916), pp. 413-20 and J. Parker, ed., 'Feet of Fines for the County of York from 1246 to 1272', *Yorkshire Archaeological Society Record Series*, LXXXII (1932).
43 Smith, I, p. 332.
44 Smith, I, p. 339.
45 A building on the east side of the lane in Thurlstone is now marked 'Top o' th' Town', but the original farm is higher up, on the opposite side of the lane.
46 Dransfield, pp. 178-79.
47 Sheffield Archives, Crewe, 616, 839.
48 R N Brownhill and J Smethurst, *The Penistone Scene* (Penistone, 1987), p. 58.
49 *The Dictionary of National Biography*, L (1897), pp. 332-33.
50 P F Ryder, *Timber-Framed Buildings in South Yorkshire* (South Yorkshire County Council County Archaeology Monograph No. 1, no date), pp. 46-61 and 78-82. David Shore of Huddersfield has made a recent study of the various Shore place-names and has come to the conclusion that they refer to rising land above a bend in a river.
51 Smith, I, p. 340.
52 Smith, I, p. 339.
53 Smith, I, p. 341; Nottinghamshire Archives, DDSR 1/17/65 and DDSR 26/97.
54 G Redmonds, *Holmfirth: place-names and settlement* (Lepton, 1994), p. 40. The cross has recently been removed from New Mill to the approximate position of its original site.
55 B English, ed., 'Yorkshire Hundred and Quo Warranto Rolls', *Yorkshire Archaeological Society Record Series*, CLI, (1996), p. 116
56 H B McCall, ed., 'Star Chamber Proceedings', II, *Yorkshire Archaeological Society Record Series*, LXIV, (1911), pp. 79-80.

57 Hunter, II, p. 361.
58 Nottinghamshire Archives DDSR 1/17/65 and 1/17/67. The Greyhound Stone has been moved for protection to Ordnance Survey grid reference SE 22770175.
59 Smith, I, p. 331; J H Brooksbank, 'The Forest of the Peak', *Transactions of the Hunter Archaeological Society*, I, 4 (1918), pp. 337-55.
60 Smith, I, p. 342.
61 Sheffield Archives, Crewe, 625; Dransfield, pp. 54 and 129; *Penistone Almanack* (1926 and 1946).
62 Sheffield Archives, Crewe, 680 and 735; *Penistone Almanack* (1927); Nicholson, pp. 27-34 quotes a detailed list of the equipment at the works in 1864.
63 Dransfield, p. 54; Nicholson, pp. 37-44.
64 Sheffield Archives, Crewe, 680, 970.
65 Nottinghamshire Archives, DDSR 26/36; Sheffield Archives, Crewe, 656.
66 Sheffield Archives, Crewe, 1554-1.
67 West Yorkshire Archives, quarter sessions indictment books, 1652; Sheffield Archives, Spencer-Stanhope, 60294/5; 60294/13; Nicholson, pp. 109-16.
68 K S B Keats-Rohan, *Domesday People: a prosopography of persons occurring in English documents, 1066-1166. 1. Domesday Book* (Woodbridge, 1999), p. 258. Lists of people purporting to have fought at the battle of Hastings (including the Bosvilles and Burdetts), such as the one which is displayed on the church wall at Dives-sur-Mer, Normandy, have long been dismissed by historians as having no supporting evidence.
69 Smith, I, p. 326; Hunter, II, pp. 350-51; *The Returns of the Poll Tax for the West Riding of Yorkshire, 1379* (Yorkshire Archaeological and Topographical Association, 1882); Warburton's map is available at Bradford, West Yorkshire Archive Service; D Hey, ed., *The Hearth Tax Returns for South Yorkshire, Ladyday 1672* (Sheffield, 1991), p. 81; C Heath, *Denby & District* (Wharncliffe Books, 2001).
70 J A Gilks, *A Neolithic Occupation Site at Castle Hill, Denby* (West Yorkshire Metropolitan County Research Committee, occasional paper, 1, 1974); Hunter, II, p. 352.
71 Hunter, II, p. 351; T Umpleby, *Water Mills and Furnaces on the Yorkshire Dearne and its Tributaries* (Wakefield Historical Publications, 2000), pp. 44 and 49.
72 Nottinghamshire Archives, DDSR 36/60. The chapel can be dated to 1229-32 because it was built while Geoffrey de Ludham was rector of Penistone.
73 Hunter, II, pp. 234-35, 353.
74 Smith, I, p. 328; Hunter, II, p. 344.
75 S Jones, 'Gunthwaite Hall Barn', *The Archaeological Journal*, 137 (1980), pp. 463-66; W E Spencer, 'Gunthwaite' in J. Addy, ed., *A Further History of Penistone* (Penistone, 1965), pp. 43-54.

Chapter 4
1 Sheffield Archives, SYC Archives, 560/F/2/1 and 3/3. See G Redmonds, *Almondbury, Places and Place-Names* (Huddersfield, 1983), pp. 28-31 and G Redmonds, 'Personal Names and Surnames in Some West Yorkshire 'Royds'', *Nomina*, 9 (1985), pp. 73-80.
2 Smith, I, p. 331.
3 Penistone churchwardens' accounts, quoted in Dransfield, pp. 162-63.
4 D Postles, 'Rural Economy on the Grits and Sandstones of the South Yorkshire Pennines, 1086-1348', *Northern History*, XV (1975), pp. 1-23.
5 R E Glasscock, ed., *The Lay Subsidy of 1334* (London, 1975), pp. 391-92.
6 Sheffield Archives, Crewe, 618.
7 J Lister, ed., 'Court Rolls of the Manor of Wakefield', III, *Yorkshire Archaeological Society Record Series*, LVII (1917), p. 2; IV, *Yorkshire Archaeological Society Record Series*, LXXVIII (1930), p. 84; Yorkshire Archaeological Society, Claremont, Leeds, MD225. I thank Dr George Redmonds for these references.
8 T W Hall, *A Descriptive Catalogue of the Bosville and Lindsay Collections* (Sheffield, 1930), p. 7, where he is recorded as William de Hatterslay.
9 D Hey, ed., *The Hearth Tax Returns for South Yorkshire, Ladyday 1672* (Sheffield, 1991).
10 University of Leeds, Brotherton Library, Wilson collection, 295/VII.
11 Borthwick Institute of Historical Research, York: Doncaster deanery wills and inventories.
12 D Hey, 'The 1801 Crop Returns for South Yorkshire', *Yorkshire Archaeological Journal*, 44 (1972), pp. 455-64.
13 S Sykes, 'Shepherds, Sheep and Gentlemen: Penistone Moorland Agriculture in the Early Nineteenth Century', in B Elliott, ed., *Aspects of Barnsley, 4* (Wharncliffe Books, 1996), pp. 189-214. Agricultural shows were held alternatively at Penistone and Wortley at the beginning of the nineteenth century. The Penistone Agricultural Society held its first show on 21 September 1854.
14 E Baines, *History, Directory and Gazetteer of the County of York, I.* West Riding (1822; reprinted 1969); J Holland, *Tour of the Don* (Sheffield, 1837), p. 62.
15 Barnsley Archives, enclosure awards.

Chapter 5
1 Revd J Hunter, *South Yorkshire: the History and Topography of the Deanery of Doncaster,* II (London, 1831), pp. 333-62. An earlier version of this chapter appeared in *Northern History*, XXXI (1995) and I am grateful to the editors for permission to reproduce it here.
2 A G Dickens, *Lollards and Protestants in the Diocese of York*, 1509-1558 (London, 1982), p. 232.
3 Revd J Hunter, *Familiae Minorum Gentium* (Harleian Society, 5 vols, 1895), pp. 40-43; *The Returns of the Poll Tax for the West Riding of Yorkshire, 1379,* Yorkshire Archaeological and Topographical Association (1882); Sheffield Archives, Crewe, 618, 620, 623, 625, 627.
4 G Redmonds, 'Amer: a rare Personal Name', *Old West Riding*, IX (1989), p. 20.

5 Sheffield Archives, Crewe, 623, 625, 705, 1542.
6 Sheffield Archives, Crewe, 735, 740, 787, 792; D. Hey, ed., *The Hearth Tax Returns for South Yorkshire, Ladyday 1672* (Sheffield, 1991), pp. 88-89.
7 Hunter, II, pp. 352-53.
8 *Yorkshire Diaries and Autobiographies in the Seventeenth and Eighteenth Centuries*, Surtees Society, LXV (1875), pp. 1-118, 351-57.
9 E G Withycombe, *The Oxford Dictionary of English Christian Names* (Oxford, 3rd edn, 1977), p. 269.
10 Withycombe, p. 100; P. Hanks and F. Hodges, *A Dictionary of First Names* (Oxford, 1990), p. 101.
11 Hunter, II, pp. 334-35. Ralph Wordsworth bought Hazlehead Hall after the death of Adam Eyre. Elias, the third son of Josias Wordsworth, became a prominent Dissenter in Sheffield, where he was the principal founder of Nether Chapel in 1715.
12 Hunter, II, pp. 346-48; in 1648 Godfrey Bosville was named one of the high court of justice for the trial of the king. However, he did not accept this office and was pardoned in 1660. *Yorkshire Diaries*, Surtees Society, LXV, pp. 18-25; cf. p. 42 on the reaction of the Rev. Adam Martindale to invitations to leave Lancashire to become minister at Penistone or at other places: 'I had more inclination to go into the West Riding of Yorkshire. The spirit of the gentrie and others in those parts was very attractive'. 266 householders in the parish of Penistone paid hearth tax in 1672, but the exempted poor were under-recorded.
13 Rev B Dale, *Yorkshire Puritanism and Early Nonconformity* (Bradford, 1909), pp. 149-51; A. G. Matthews, *Calamy Revised* (Oxford, 1934), p. 472.
14 Hunter, II, pp. 352-53.
15 Dale, pp. 149-51.
16 Yorkshire Diaries, pp. 23, 35, 51, 57, 104.
17 J H Turner, ed., *The Rev. Oliver Heywood, B. A., 1630-1702: his Autobiography, Diaries, Anecdotes and Event Books*, I-IV (Brighouse, 1881-85).
18 A Gordon, *Freedom After Ejection, 1690-92* (Manchester, 1917); *Yorkshire Diaries*, pp. 119-62; Sheffield Archives, Crewe, 845.
19 Hunter, I (1828), pp. 290-92.
20 Sheffield Archives, Crewe, 858-61.
21 H J Morehouse, ed., *Extracts from the Diary of the Revd Robert Meeke* (London and Huddersfield, 1874), pp. 20-24.
22 Sheffield Archives, Crewe, 870; Hunter, II, pp. 339-40.
23 West Yorkshire Archive Service, Wakefield: quarter sessions records, order books.
24 Hunter, II, p. 362, note.
25 Dr Williams's Library, London: Evans mss, 34-4.
26 West Yorkshire Archive Service, QSI/39/10. Richard Micklethwaite of Ingbirchworth, gentleman, also served on the grand jury.
27 J N Dransfield, *A History of the Parish of Penistone* (Penistone, 1906), pp. 150-51.
28 S L Ollard and P C Walker, *Archbishop Herring's Visitation Records, 1743*, Yorkshire Archaeological Society Record Series, LXXV (1929), p. 5; Borthwick Institute of Historical Research, York: Archbishop Drummond's visitation returns, 1764.
29 *Yorkshire Diaries*, pp. 249-51.

Chapter 6
1 University of Leeds, Wilson collection, XXXIII, 149d.
2 Wilson collection, VII (78 to 116).
3 Hunter, II, p. 335.
4 Reproduced in Dransfield, p. 281.
5 D Hey, ed., *The Hearth Tax Returns for South Yorkshire, Ladyday 1672* (Sheffield, 1991), p. 85.
6 Public Record Office, WO 30/48.
7 Nottinghamshire Record Office, Mellish, 63-2.
8 J Addy, 'Penistone Grammar School in the Eighteenth Century', *Yorkshire Archaeological Society*, XXXIX (1957), pp. 356-63.
9 H. Heaton, *The Yorkshire Woollen and Worsted Industries* (Oxford, 1920), p. 136 note.
10 D Defoe, *A Tour through the Whole Island of Great Britain* (London: Everyman edition, 1962), pp. 81-82.
11 Borthwick Institute of Historical Research, York, Pontefract Deanery wills and inventories, proved June 1689. See also G.D. Ramsay, 'The Distribution of the Cloth Industry in 1561-2', *English Historical Review*, LVII (1942), pp. 361-69.
12 Heaton, pp. 79-80.
13 G D Ramsay, 'The Distribution of the Cloth Industry in 1561-2', *English Historical Review*, LVII (1942), pp. 361-69.
14 G E Dawson and L Kennedy-Skipton, *Elizabethan Handwriting, 1500-1650* (London: Faber, 1966), p. 66. The original document is in the Folger Library, Washington, USA.
15 Borthwick Institute of Historical Research, York, probate inventories, Doncaster deanery.
16 Sheffield Archives, Spencer Stanhope, 60505.
17 Sheffield Archives, Crewe, 969. Twenty-two of the signatories signed with a mark.
18 i.e. sample.
19 Sheffield Archives, Crewe, 970.
20 John Platt's journal for March 1763 is available on microfilm in Rotherham Archives and Local Studies Library and is quoted extensively in J D Pott's booklet, *Platt of Rotherham, Mason-Architects, 1700-1810* (Sheffield, 1959).
21 Hunter, II, p. 335.
22 See note 20.
23 J H Wood, *Remarkable Occurrences, Interesting Dates and Curious Information (Local and General)*, (Penistone, 1890), p. 15; J. Addy, ed., *A Further History of Penistone* (Penistone, 1965), p. 4.

24 I thank Dr Stephen Caunce for these references.
25 P Crossland, 'Penistone Market' in Brian Elliott. ed., *Aspects of Barnsley, 3* (Wharncliffe Books, 1995), pp. 230-40.
26 J Addy, 'Penistone Grammar School, 1392-1700', *Yorkshire Archaeological Society,* XXXIX (1958), pp. 508-14.
27 See note 26.
28 Sheffield Archives, Crewe, 1092.

Chapter 7

1   Sheffield Archives, Crewe, 662; Spencer-Stanhope collection, 60217.
2   'A Dyurnall, or Catalogue of all my Accions and Expenses from the 1st January, 1646[7] – Adam Eyre', *Surtees Society,* LXV (1875), p. 40, 69.
3   D Hey, *Packmen, Carriers and Packhorse Roads: Trade and Communications in North Derbyshire and South Yorkshire* (Ashbourne, second edition, 2001), pp. 25-35; H Smith, *The Guide Stoops of the Dark Peak* (Sheffield, privately printed, 1999).
4   W B Crump, *Huddersfield Highways Down the Ages* (Huddersfield, 1949), pp. 144-48.
5   On saltways see Hey, *Packmen,* pp. 110-16.
6. T S Willan, *The Early History of the Don Navigation* (Manchester, 1965), p. 147.
7   *Journal of the House of Commons,* XXIII, p.568.
8   *Journal of the House of Commons,* XXII, p. 805; 'Yorkshire Diaries and Autobiographies in the Seventeenth and Eighteenth Centuries', *Surtees Society,* LXV (1875), p.315.
9. *Journal of the House of Commons,* XXIII, p. 568.
10 *Journal of the House of Commons,* XXIII, pp. 575 and 613.
11 *Journal of the house of Commons,* XXIII, p. 583.
12 *Journal of the House of Commons,* XXIII, p. 613.
13 *Journal of the House of Commons,* XXIX, pp. 173 and 223.
14 Manchester Waterworks boundary stones still mark their property at Saltersbrook, close to the old highway.
15 The initials IWB were carved by Isaac Watt Boulton of Ashton-under-Lyne, a railway engineer with an interest in early forms of transport; see A R Bennett, *Chronicles of Boulton's Siding* (Newton Abbott, 1974). I thank Trevor Lodge for this reference.
16 Sheffield Archives, Fairbank collection, Pen 31S.
17 Wakefield, West Yorkshire Archive Service, quarter sessions records, Rotherham, 1828.
18 Revd J F Prince, *Silkstone: the History and Topography of the Parish of Silkstone* (Penistone, 1922), p. 56.
19 'Yorkshire Diaries and Autobiographies in the Seventeenth and Eighteenth Centuries', *Surtees Society,* LXV (1875), p. 262.
20 West Yorkshire Archive Service, Penistone parish registers.
21 Copies of posters in author's collection.
22 Bradford, West Yorkshire Archive Service, Warburton's map.
23 *Journal of the House of Commons,* XXIX, pp. 173 and 223.
24 *Journal of the House of Commons,* XXX, p, 230.
25 H Smith, *Mortimer Road: the turnpike that failed* (Sheffield, privately published, 1993).
26 University of Leeds, Brotherton Library, Wilson, CLIX, f. 71.
27 Wilson, CLIX, f. 70.
28 Curiously, a similar 'Take Off' stone stands near Postbridge, Dartmoor.
29 British Library, Lansdowne, 913.
30 J Holland, *Tour of the Don* (Sheffield, 1837), p. 78.
31 B Jackson, *Cawthorne, 1790-1990* (Cawthorne, 1991), p. 40.

Chapter 8

1   D Hey, ed., *The Militia Men of the Barnsley District, 1806: an analysis of the Staincross militia returns* (Sheffield, 1998; available on microfiche from the Sheffield and District Family History Society).
2   H Heaton, *The Yorkshire Woollen and Worsted Industries* (Oxford, 1920); W B Crump and G Ghorbal, *History of the Huddersfield Woollen Industry* (Huddersfield, 1935 and 1967 reprint).
3   L Caffyn, *Workers' Housing in West Yorkshire, 1750-1920* (London, 1986), pp. 18, 44, 150.
4   E Baines, *History, Directory and Gazetteer of the County of York: 1. West Riding* (1822 and 1969 reprint); C Heath, *Denby & District* (Wharncliffe Books, 2001), pp. 100-1.
5   Ordnance Survey grid reference 23900923.
6   T Umpleby, *Water Mills and Furnaces on the Yorkshire Dearne and Its Tributaries* (Wakefield Historical Publications, 2000), pp. 10, 39-51; T Schmoller, *Sheffield papermakers: three centuries of papermaking in the Sheffield area* (Sheffield, 1992).
7   Ordnance Survey grid reference 20190798; Umpleby, p. 39. A group of buildings at Birds Edge is marked on a 1776 map of the intended turnpike road from Penistone to Huddersfield (Bretton Hall archives). See Dransfield, p. 136 for the two Elihu Dickensons, clothier and tanner, of High Flatts.
8   Umpleby, p. 42. Baines's 1822 *Directory* also lists Charles Wood & Son, fancy manufacturers of Denby Dale, and Sam. Wood & Co., woollen manufacturers of Ingbirchworth.
9   C Heath, *Denby & District* (Wharncliffe Books, 2001), pp. 183-86.
10 C Heath, *Denby & District* (Wharncliffe Books, 2001), p. 147.
11 C Heath, *Denby & District* (Wharncliffe Books, 2001), pp. 126-32. Tedber, Tedbar or Tedbah is derived from the Biblical name, Tebah, the brother of Abraham (Genesis, 22, v. 20-24).
12 K Lindley, *Chapels and Meeting Houses* (London, 1969), pp. 61-62.
13 D Bostwick, 'The Denby Dale Pies: an illustrative narrative history', *Folk Life, Journal of Ethnological Studies,* 26 (1987-88), pp. 12-42.

14 V Nicholson, *Upper Don Watermills* (Sheffield, 2001), pp. 45-66.

15 Nicholson, pp. 67-78.

16 Nicholson, pp. 79-90.

17 Sheffield Archives, WBC 44 and the printed *Catalogue of the Family Papers of John Wainwright of Thurlstone*.

18 J Holland, *Tour of the Don* (Sheffield, 1837), p. 55.

19 Public Record Office, HO/129/506; A E Beard, 'A Short History of Netherfield Congregational Church, Penistone, 1786 to 1900' (privately produced, no date).

20 D Bayliss, ed., *Industrial History of South Yorkshire* (Association for Industrial Archaeology, 1995), p. 56.

21 Bullhouse Colliery ephemera in my possession.

22 *Barnsley Chronicle*, 17 May 1985.

23 *Report of the Royal Commission on Children's Employment* (London, 1842).

24 Typescript copy in Barnsley Library, Local Studies Department.

25 J Kenworthy, *Early History of Stocksbridge and District* (Deepcar, 1928); Stocksbridge & District Society, *Around Stocksbridge* (Stroud, 1996); J. Branston, *History of Stocksbridge* (Stocksbridge, no date).

26 P Crossland, 'Thurgoland Wire Mills' in B Elliott, ed., *Aspects of Barnsley, 2* (Wharncliffe Books, 1994), pp. 215-28.

27 Nicholson, pp. 145-50.

28 Nicholson, pp. 141-44. The inventory of the personal estate of Robert Camm of Roughbirchworth, taken on 2 October 1728, included 'Shop - Wire & all working tools, £1'.

29 Nicholson, pp. 131-40.

30 T Coleman, *The Railway Navvies* (Harmondsworth, 1968), pp. 115-38.

31 C Heath, *Denby & District* (Wharncliffe Books, 2001), pp. 151-52.

32 On the Race Common quarry, see Sheffield Archives, SYC Archives 178/B.

33 Holland, p. 62.

34 Dransfield, pp. 172, 343.

35 This and the following paragraph is based on Dransfield, J H Wood, *Remarkable Occurrences* (Penistone, 1886), the set of *Penistone Almanacks* at Barnsley Library, Local Studies Department, and R N Brownhill and J Smethurst, *The Penistone Scene* (Penistone, 1987).

36 Nicholson, pp. 117-30.

37 N Pevsner, *The Buildings of England: Yorkshire, West Riding* (Harmondsworth, 1959), p. 392.

38 Dr A C J Wilson, 'Fifty Years in a Moorland Practice', *British Medical Journal*, 1 January 1927.

Chapter 9

1 Public Record Office, MAF 32/327/1152, part 2.

2 A set can be seen in Barnsley Archives.

3 Barnsley Archives, microfilms.